WITNESS OF THE LIGHT

WITNESS OF THE LIGHT

A Photographic Journey in the Footsteps of the American Prophet Joseph Smith

Text and Photography by
SCOT FACER PROCTOR

Edited by Maurine Jensen Proctor
Designed by Kent Ware

Deseret Book Company
Salt Lake City, Utah

© 1991 Scot Facer Proctor

All rights reserved. No part of this book may be reproduced in any form or by any means without permission in writing from the publisher, Deseret Book Company, P.O. Box 30178, Salt Lake City, Utah 84130. This work is not an official publication of The Church of Jesus Christ of Latter-day Saints. The views expressed herein are the responsibility of the author and do not necessarily represent the position of the Church or of Deseret Book Company.

Deseret Book is a registered trademark of Deseret Book Company.

Library of Congress Cataloging-in-Publication

Proctor, Scot Facer, 1956–
    Witness of the light : a photographic journey in the footsteps of the American prophet Joseph Smith / Scot Facer Proctor.
    p. cm.
    ISBN 0-87579-389-4 (hard)
    ISBN 1-57345-056-1 (paper)
    1. Smith, Joseph, 1805–1844—Pictorial works. 2. Church of Jesus Christ of Latter-day Saints—Presidents—Biography—Pictorial works. 3. Mormon Church—Presidents—Biography—Pictorial works. I. Title.
BX8695.S6P74   1991
289.3'092—dc20
[B]   91-71335
                                                                                 CIP

Printed in the United States of America

10 9 8 7 6 5 4 3 2 1

CONTENTS

PERSONAL NOTES

Page 6

PROLOGUE

Page 10

1 FOUNDATIONS OF FAITH: THE NEW ENGLAND HERITAGE

Page 12

2 LIGHTS FROM THE HEAVENS AND A VOICE FROM THE DUST

Page 36

3 OUT OF POVERTY: A HOUSE FOR THE SON OF GOD

Page 84

4 MISSOURI: LOOKING FOR THE HIGH GROUND THROUGH THE REFINER'S FIRE

Page 116

5 NAUVOO: A PATTERN FOR BUILDING THE CITY OF GOD

Page 156

EPILOGUE

Page 204

NOTES

Page 206

PERSONAL NOTES

Behind every picture in this book is an adventure, both historical and recent. There is something very compelling to me about "composing" a picture, much as a musician would compose a line of music. I was doing that very thing one early morning on Dairy Hill in Vermont, about two hundred and fifty yards from the birthplace of the Prophet Joseph Smith. My wife, Maurine, and baby, Mariah, were back at camp, and I was out to capture some New England fog and fields. I had set up the big Pentax 6x7 camera on the tripod and was crossing a rail fence to capture the beautiful scenery in the valley below. On an instant the Spirit whispered to me to run back to the road and set up the camera—now! Familiar with the voice, I obeyed immediately, without hesitation, and got ready for whatever was to come. I had no sooner set up the camera than an orphan patch of thick fog blew gently across the road in front of me, blocking the sun and creating a wonderful effect. I bracketed the shot, having only enough time to take one perfect exposure. Within thirty seconds the fog had vanished into the atmosphere and the experience was over. It was exhilarating! The Spirit whispered again, "You will use that one." It is the cover.

I have long desired to compose a set of pictures into an oratorio of light on the Restoration and the life of this marvelous man, Joseph Smith. I have traveled untold thousands of miles back and forth to places of import in the history of The Church of Jesus Christ of Latter-day Saints, doing what I call "photographic essays" on the Restoration. I have exposed many more pictures than I could afford, always thinking I would capture something never seen before.

I grew up a boy of the land, like Joseph in many ways. Our family had wonderful traditions, which included "pulling sticks" every Fourth of July. When I reached my full stature, I ended up the same physical size as Joseph, to the pound and the inch. Though I know he could beat me, I would still like to pull sticks with him.

I don't just research history; I try to feel it and hear it and taste it. I have slept in every season on the ground under the open heavens at nearly every site. I slept through an all-night Pennsylvania downpour at Harmony, never getting wet, safe under a friendly pine tree. I have slept on the Smith Farm in Manchester many times, and at the base of the Hill Cumorah. I have slept on the original temple acres in Independence. I have sung a solo of all seven verses of "A Poor Wayfaring Man of Grief" in the Carthage jail. I have read nearly all the revelations of the Doctrine and Covenants aloud in the various places where they were received. I have waded in the waters of the sacred Susquehanna River.

One cold mid-October night, I wanted to capture the movement of the constellations around the north star on Tower Hill at Adam-ondi-Ahman. Being alone on the trip, and yet not "alone," I set up the camera in a vertical mode, locked the tripod tightly with the center focus on Polaris, and opened the shutter. The exposure

Above: Early morning sun at Adam-ondi-Ahman, Missouri, near where I slept in the weeds to get the star shot. The frost is thick upon the fields in the valley below. There is a powerful spirit here that elicits feelings of quiet in my heart. I grew up on a farm that looks similar to this place.

Left: Scovill Bakery in Nauvoo, Illinois. I love this little building. I love the people who work here. And I love the cookies they have given me on many occasions. I have spent hours just walking the streets of Nauvoo, sometimes at 4:00 in the morning or 11:00 at night. I have learned much from nature and the wind here. I love to walk in the footsteps of this great prophet, Joseph Smith.

would take seven and a half hours to complete and would use one whole camera battery. I laid out my sleeping bag on a waterproof cloth over the thick weeds next to the camera and tried to sleep. No sooner had I put my head on the ground than I heard six coyotes in the great field below and two others closer, separated by a small draw between them. I know about animals because I grew up in the woods of Missouri; our home was surrounded by nearly two hundred acres of oak, elm, hickory, and dogwood. The coyotes were decidedly curious that I was there. I was concerned that after I fell asleep the coyotes might come too close and bump the tripod, ruining the exposure. The animals howled and yapped and barked and moved closer. Two large owls then entered the scene, landing above me in the barren walnut trees. They hooted, assuring me that they would keep watch and warn me of the hungry coyotes. I snuggled deeper into the sleeping bag, the frost already gathering on my face, and silently slept until 4:30 A.M. The owls stayed by me, the coyotes never came, the picture was wonderful. I thought: Surely Joseph slept out in this same place and heard similar sounds. I wonder what he thought.

One summer night, on the trail of Zion's Camp, in Parke County, Indiana, we were trying to find a place to park our Suburban and sleep for the night. We had a wonderful bed in the back and a place for the baby, but this night we could not find an adequate place to park. It was nearly 11:00, and I was tired of driving. Photographers have to be up before sunrise to catch the morning light. Finally we reached the Lyford Bible Church, which seemed to have a perfect parking lot hidden in the back. I pulled in, we cracked the windows for air, and then we settled down for a short summer's sleep.

Within minutes the Suburban came under siege by squadrons of mosquitoes, which began to enter the vehicle from both sides. They were not coming for me or Mariah—just for Maurine. They seemed to think her insect repellent was a sweet nectar. After three hours of the buzzing and eating, Maurine cried, "I can't take it anymore!" I told Maurine that they weren't so bad; I wasn't bothered by them at all. "Just go to sleep," I said wisely. Surely Maurine couldn't have given more blood safely to the Red Cross that night, and the mosquitoes could barely fly in the morning. I chuckled a little and wrote it off to experience. Weeks later we were in Nauvoo, and Maurine must have built up an immunity to insects by then. We slept north of Temple Square, behind the Raymond Store. I was so tired this night, with seven thousand miles behind us on this shoot. Maurine and Mariah quickly fell asleep, but I could not. The sound of insect bombers was everywhere. I was being attacked by the original swamp mosquitoes of the Mississippi River. I tried to be patient. I tried not to talk. I tried to be brave. After three hours, I had had enough. I woke up Maurine and said, "I can't take this anymore. I'm being eaten alive!" "Just go to sleep," she whispered, not even coherent enough to remember Lyford, Indiana. So, I know this small aspect of the trials of the early Saints, and I did not fare so well!

Ninety-eight percent of the pictures in this book were shot on Fujichrome 50D and 100D Professional Transparency Film. I love the freshness of the greens in the pictures and the accuracy of the colors in general. I have used a flash only three times in these photos, all the rest being taken in natural light. I did not use any filters except an occasional polarizer in very bright light. I have tried to avoid all power lines, automobiles, people, jet streams, street signs, asphalt roads, and any other marks of our modern world, trying to create a timeless symphony of light images. Sometimes this is difficult. I photographed one low-lying sunset in Jackson County, where I was urged by the Spirit to hurry; within five minutes eleven vibrant jet streams crossed the sky. Joseph didn't see those, and I hope you won't either.

I love the Lord Jesus Christ. I love His Prophet, Joseph Smith. I have studied Joseph and tried to discover his paths for twenty years. I have never tired of this. I can't remember a day in the past thirteen years when I haven't pulled out a primary source or commentary and learned something new about the early days of the Church. Every boy has his heroes; mine became Joseph and Hyrum Smith, Parley Parker Pratt, Lucy Mack Smith, Brigham Young, Eliza R. Snow, Sarah Melissa Granger Kimball. I desire to honor them in this book, arranging a piece that was technologically impossible in their day.

My thanks are many, and the plates are nearly full. My deepest thanks go to the Lord, who has taught me that I am an unprofitable servant, that no matter how much I do, He immediately blesses me, and I am ever in His debt. My wife, Maurine Ann, is the completion of my soul. She has been the Polaris in my life, a steady, sure star, full of faith in her husband and in the Lord. She has never wavered in her belief that I could accomplish this project, or any other. Oh, how I love her! She edited the book as we sat at home in our office and has offered deep insight and direction throughout. Many a day we have been in tears as we read to each other from the journals and accounts of the past. Kent Ware, Sheri Dew, and Ron Millett have been like night-criers in the Colonies, telling everyone with powerful voices of the coming of this project, with unwavering belief in its importance. Sheri has really gone out of her way to get this project off the ground at Deseret Book, pushing ahead based on feelings and hunches, for which I am deeply grateful. Kent is a remarkable art director and designer and has really been the instrument of balance in the book. He is delightful to work with, and to him is much credit due. I am grateful for Jack Lyon's masterful copy editing. He has added great clarity and fluidity to the book. My parents, Paul and Martha Proctor, have probably permanently indented their wood floors with the pressure of their knees in prayer for me during the project. They are so dear, and I thank them profusely for their undying belief in their youngest son. Our ten children have been patient and have sacrificed day in and night out to let me work uninterrupted to do the research and finish the manuscript. I also thank the scores of missionary couples over the years who have been kind to me.

Just a few weeks after Joseph Smith was first visited by the Angel Moroni and given knowledge of the ancient record of the Nephites, his beloved elder brother Alvin was taken tragically and suddenly in death. This was devastating to Joseph. Shortly before Alvin died, he told Joseph to do all in his power to bring forth the record and to be obedient to the Lord. Just a few weeks after I signed the contract to do this book, my beloved elder brother, Kirk, was taken tragically and suddenly in death. This was devastating to me. Shortly before he died, though the imminence of his death was unknown to either of us, Kirk told me to do all in my power to produce this book in a manner that would be pleasing to the Lord and to be diligent and true. I lovingly dedicate this book to Alvin Smith and Kirk F. Proctor and to the Prophet Joseph Smith, who is also my friend and my brother.

PROLOGUE

What is the world to make of a man who declares that the heavens have burst open and knowledge of God has been given again to humanity? that he has been visited by an angel who has given him an ancient record testifying of Jesus Christ—and then actually produces that record? that he has seen God the Eternal Father and His Son Jesus Christ, who have told him that none of the creeds of the world are correct?

Joseph Smith was the man, and, frankly, the world was puzzled. Joseph himself said: "I don't blame anyone for not believing my history. If I had not experienced what I have, I could not have believed it myself."[1] Still, he testified: "I had actually seen a light, and in the midst of that light I saw two Personages, and they did in reality speak to me; and though I was hated and persecuted for saying that I had seen a vision, yet it was true. . . . I knew it, and I knew that God knew it, and I could not deny it, neither dared I do it; at least I knew that by so doing I would offend God, and come under condemnation."[2]

The Lord had told Amos in the Old Testament that he would do nothing save he revealed it unto his servants the prophets (see Amos 3:7), and now He had opened a new dispensation by revealing himself to a prophet again, this time to a young man in New York with a common name like Joseph Smith.

To his detractors he was a fraud. They let out one long holler of derision at his claim. As one said, "I thought the man either crazed or a very shallow impostor."[3]

Still, in this world, crazed and shallow imposters show up every day, but they do not have the magnetic power to capture the dedication of the people around them. For the doctrines Joseph taught, people were willing again and again to leave a trail of their scattered possessions behind them, willing to suffer death for the faith he taught them.

To his disciples, he was a prophet, God's chosen instrument to restore the gospel of Jesus Christ with all its keys, principles, and ordinances. One of these, Parley P. Pratt, said, "There was something connected with the serene and steady penetrating glance of his eye, as if he would penetrate the deepest abyss of the human heart, gaze into eternity, penetrate the heavens, and comprehend all worlds."[4]

Joseph was by any account someone to be reckoned with. In the early summer of 1844, Josiah Quincy, who would shortly become the cultured mayor of Boston, visited the city of Nauvoo and spent a few hours with the Prophet Joseph Smith. Quincy asked questions about the faith, toured the city with the Prophet himself, and then went home to write an essay about the man he had met, sizing up the Prophet in these words: "It is by no means improbable that some future text-book, for the use of generations yet unborn, will contain a question something like this: What historical American of the nineteenth century has exerted the most powerful influence upon the destinies of his countrymen? And it is by no means impossible that the answer to that interrogatory may be thus written: *Joseph Smith, the Mormon Prophet.* And the reply, absurd as it doubtless seems to most men now living, may be an obvious commonplace to their descendants. History deals in surprises and paradoxes quite as startling as this."[5]

To understand Joseph Smith and the revelations he received, we have to take him at his word—that he was a prophet. Scholars of the Bible had long been puzzled by a verse in Acts that declared that Jesus Christ would be sent again to the children of men after the "restitution of all things." (Acts 3:21.) How could there be a restitution unless there had been a falling away?

Though much of the Christian world believed that the gospel had continued unbroken since Jesus Christ had given it in his mortal ministry, the Lord told Joseph something different. He said the gospel of Jesus Christ and His saving mission was established before the foundation of the earth and that it had been known by people in every dispensation. (A dispensation is a time when the church of God with its ordinances and revelations is upon the earth. It is followed by a period of apostasy brought on by wickedness.)

When the Savior's apostles were preaching the gospel after His resurrection, they were aware that there would be another complete falling away from the truth. Paul wrote to the Thessalonians, warning them not to be deceived about the second coming of the Lord, "for that day shall not come, except there come a falling away first." (2 Thessalonians 2:3.)

So how was God to usher in His great, last dispensation before the Second Coming? For unlike other dispensations, this one would not end in apostasy but would usher in the Millennium, the thousand years of peace, with Jesus Christ Himself reigning as King of kings and Lord of lords. How was a people to be prepared to meet the Savior when He came? An unwavering, unchanging God would do it, of course, the way He has always done it—by giving a prophet knowledge and authority of God. We cannot comprehend the Lord or His ways unless He reveals Himself to us.

Humanity, left to itself, tries to press forward, but everywhere we turn we find that our best ideas are no more than promising puffs of smoke blown away on the wind. They warm us for a while and then come to nothing. Who, then, will give us the knowledge to fill our souls with light? No one in this confused world.

But that knowledge came from the Lord, breaking the long silence from the heavens, when He visited fourteen-year-old Joseph Smith in 1820. The world responded as it would to anything truly novel: with disbelief and rage. Of such people the Lord asked, "Wherefore murmur ye because ye shall receive more of my word?" (2 Nephi 29:8.) Still there were thousands and then millions who had ears to hear.

So this book catches only a few glimpses of a true modern-day prophet, the light shed upon him, and the price he paid for it. It does not explore deeply the revolutionary doctrines he taught. For these, the interested reader must pursue the Book of Mormon, the Doctrine and Covenants, and the Pearl of Great Price, three formidable volumes of scripture no uninspired person could have produced.

This is the last great dispensation when the gospel is upon the earth, the Dispensation of the Fullness of Times, and this knowledge is given freely to humanity to prepare them to meet the Lord. Given the doctrines revealed by Joseph Smith and the faith to live them, surely a people can be prepared.

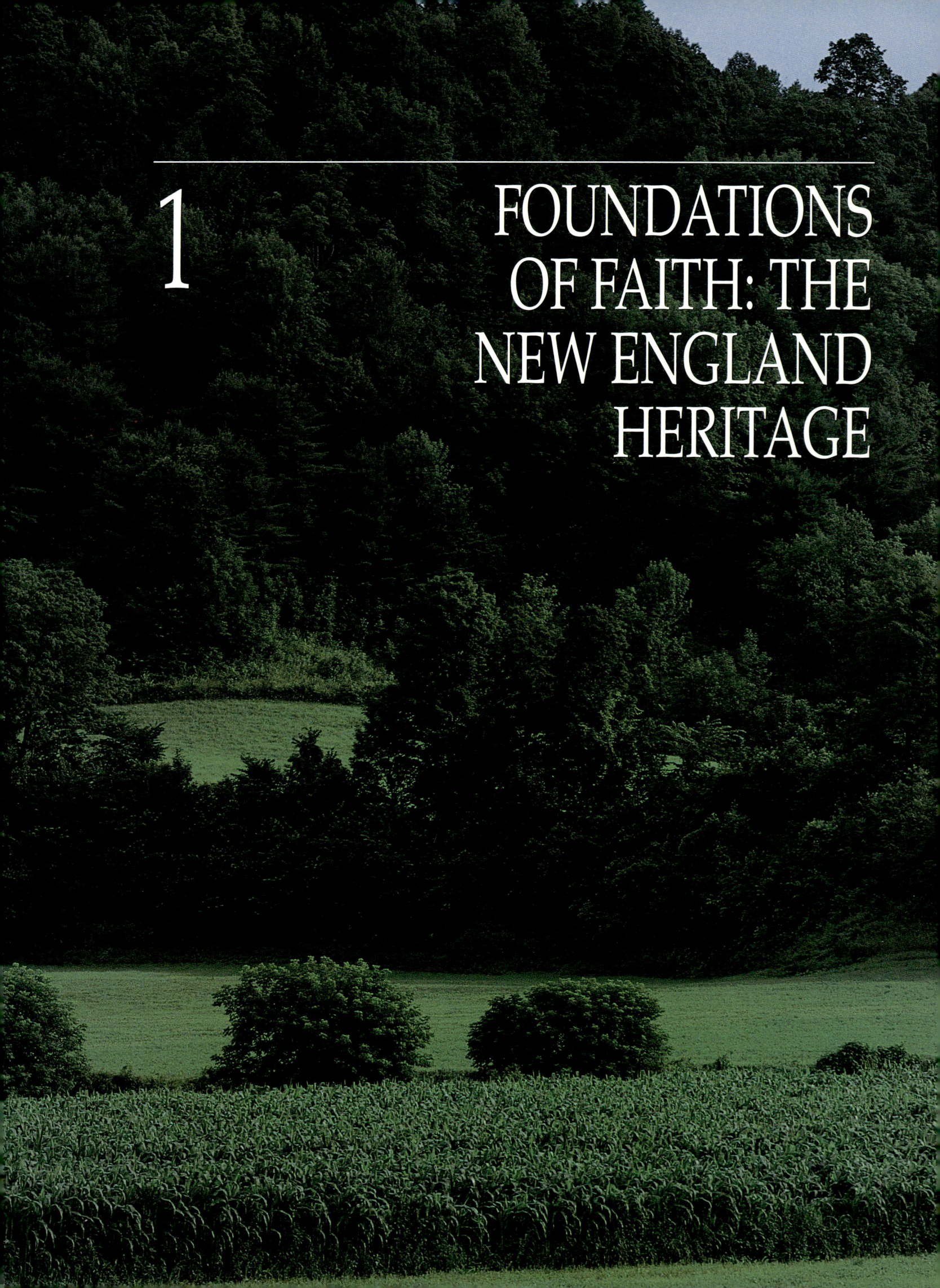

1 FOUNDATIONS OF FAITH: THE NEW ENGLAND HERITAGE

The golden-yellow leaves of the sugar maple begin their downward glide to the ground. The wind is gentle but sure as each tree forms a cover quilted by nature to capture the moisture of the oncoming winter. The constant chattering of the gray squirrels indicates the gathering—a time to prepare for the change of the seasons.

In an obscure spot in Vermont, in 1805, came a similar change of seasons. Golden maple leaves, yes, but much more. The world slumbered: "For the Lord hath poured out upon you the spirit of deep sleep, and hath closed your eyes: the prophets and your rulers, the seers hath he covered." (Isaiah 29:10.) But the breezes were blowing in a new awakening. The earth itself and all her inhabitants were about to enter a new season. It was not marked on the calendar or announced in the newspaper, but after centuries of silence from the heavens, when humanity claimed that the Lord had grown quiet, something was about to happen.

Pages 12–13: Lush countryside touched by morning light as fog begins to break up around a farm on a hillside near Tunbridge, Vermont. Twenty-four-year-old Joseph Smith, father of the future Prophet, met and married twenty-year-old Lucy Mack in this area, and they spent the first six years of their marriage here.

Left: Line of sugar maples standing as sentinels marking the way to the birthplace of the Prophet Joseph Smith on Dairy Hill in the township of Sharon, Windsor County, Vermont. The young Smith family rented a farm here for about two years from Solomon Mack, Lucy's father.

Above: Queen Anne's Lace grows wild on the hills of Sharon, Vermont. The Smiths tried everything in their power to tame the land of New England, growing crops and likely tapping the maples for their sweet extract. These were times of survival and striving to make ends meet.

Remnant of old wall by "turnpike" that passes through property of Solomon Mack, about 1/4 mile from birthplace of the Prophet Joseph Smith, circa 1780–1800. Natives report that this turnpike led from Boston to Montreal. Surely the shadows of the trees dance across the mossy rocks in the same way they did two hundred years ago.

That fall the Lucy Mack and Joseph Smith Sr. family were expecting a baby. The new nation was not yet three decades old. Thomas Jefferson was president. Politicians of the day freely acknowledged the hand of God in forming the nation. And everywhere men and women were trying to tame a wilderness, where food for their families depended on their crops, and failure was as close as tomorrow's turn in the weather.

The Smiths struggled to make a living. Windsor County, Vermont, was beautiful and harsh. It was inviting and unrelenting. It was a land of green mountains and stone fences.

Religion was on everyone's mind. Many had come from the Old World to escape the captivity of doctrines and traditions that imprisoned free conscience and the Spirit. Many were searching for a restoration of New Testament Christianity, and those who earnestly looked for it were popularly known as "seekers." Most were looking for opportunities—great opportunities—spiritual ones and more.

Rocks are gathered from the fields of New England to build walls and boundaries and to make room for tender crops. The fall leaves grace the top of this old section of fence located in the Tunbridge Gore area of Vermont. A "gore" is a piece of land not included in original surveys, usually because it was too rugged or inaccessible. The Smiths lived in "the gore."

Joseph Smith's forebears had been in New England five generations. With a combined ethic of hard work, strict moral conscience, and Yankee independence, they had distinguished themselves and were a family of some means. They show a history of religious yearning, a desire to know the Lord, and a discontent for the religions of the day.

The Smiths' independence of thought is indicated in a public document three of them signed in 1796, declaring that it was "Contrary to the dictates of our consciences, to pay money . . . towards the support of any teacher of any different denomination whatever."[1]

That was nine years before the Prophet's birth. Grandfather Asael Smith had had intimations from the Spirit that a great work was yet to come to the earth. He told a grandson "that he always knew that God was going to raise up some branch of his family to be a great benefit to mankind,"[2] "that something would turn up in his family that would revolutionize the world."[3]

Above: Old Royalton Church, circa 1797. The Smiths would have known this church and been familiar with many of the people who attended here. Faith and religion were in the mind of Lucy Mack Smith and her husband, Joseph. They wanted with all their hearts to find the ancient order of the gospel that Jesus Himself had established.

Right: The Green Mountains of Vermont, where fog and light weave among the hollows, ridges, and draws. The Smiths knew this country well. Brigham Young, Oliver Cowdery, Heber C. Kimball, David Patten, and Newell K. Whitney, who would one day become prominent leaders in the church Joseph Smith would restore, were all natives of Vermont.

The woman preparing in the fall of 1805 for the birth of her fourth child had been prepared long before for the kind of man he would be.

Three years before, Lucy Mack Smith had developed tuberculosis. Burning with fever and so weak she could not abide even a footfall in her room, she was given only a few more days to live. Through the dim haze of sickness, she worried whether she would die, for then, as she later wrote, "I did not consider myself ready for such an awful event, inasmuch as I knew not the ways of Christ; besides, there appeared to be a dark and lonesome chasm between myself and the Savior, which I dared not attempt to pass."[4] Her husband, Joseph, cried, "Oh, Lucy! my wife! my wife! you must die! The doctors have given you up, and all say you cannot live."[5]

She wrote: "I then looked to the Lord and begged and pleaded with him to spare my life in order that I might bring up my children and be a comfort to my husband. My mind was much agitated during the whole night. . . .

"During this night I made a solemn covenant with God that if He would let me live I would endeavor to serve him according to the best of my abilities. Shortly after this I heard a voice say to me, 'Seek, and ye shall find; knock, and it shall be opened unto you. Let your heart be comforted; ye believe in God, believe also in me.'

"In a few moments my mother came in and, looking upon me, she said, 'Lucy, you are better.'"[6]

Lucy had been miraculously healed but spiritually disquieted. She spent much of her time reading the Bible, searching for the key to having "a change of heart." The desire to have this change come upon her consumed every thought. She wanted to become a member of a church, but this presented a dilemma for her: "If I remain a member of no church, all religious people will say I am of the world, and if I join some one of the different denominations, all the rest will say I am in error."[7]

Studying with all diligence to keep her covenant with the Lord, at last she came to a conclusion: "I said in my heart that there was not then upon earth the religion which I sought."[8]

Joseph Smith Sr. had also been prepared to father a prophet. During the early childhood of young Joseph, his father had received seven prophetic dreams teaching him that a great work was about to come forth upon the land and that his family would take part in it.

In one of these dreams, he was led by a guide who brought him to a pleasant valley where a tree stood that bore fruit of an unearthly, dazzling whiteness. Eating it, Joseph Sr. found it "delicious beyond description."⁹ Joseph shared the heavenly fruit with his family. He asked the guide the meaning of the fruit and was answered that "it was the pure love of God, shed abroad in the hearts of all those who love him, and keep his commandments."¹⁰

Well had the Lord spoken of such a family through the Old Testament prophet Joel: "And it shall come to pass afterward, that I will pour out my spirit upon all flesh; and your sons and your daughters shall prophesy, your old men shall dream dreams, your young men shall see visions." (Joel 2:28.)

Left: Fall touches a stand of paper birch and white oak in a forest in the Tunbridge Gore near the place where son Hyrum was born to Lucy and Joseph Smith. All the Smiths worked hard, eking out a living in this environment where the growing seasons were short and the risk of losing crops to a change of the weather was high.

Above: Old Vermont schoolhouse near Sharon, Vermont, where Joseph Smith Sr. may have taught school during the winter months. Joseph Sr. was described as "six feet, two inches high, . . . very straight, and remarkably well proportioned. . . . He was very strong and active. In his younger days he was famed as a wrestler, and, Jacob like, he never wrestled with but one man whom he could not throw."¹¹

Above: Beautiful flowers in their splendor grace the area where the Prophet Joseph Smith was born. The township line of Sharon and Royalton ran right through the middle of the Smiths' cabin, but it is believed that Joseph was born on the Sharon side.

Right: Solid granite shaft 38 1/2 feet high placed at the site of the birthplace of the Prophet on the centennial of his birth, December 23, 1905. The monument stands tall and strong amid the trees in this rural spot in Vermont. Each foot of the shaft represents one year of Joseph Smith's brief life.

The earth made her turns, and the darkest night of the year arrived. In ancient times at the winter solstice, people crept to the edge of mountains to watch the sky, praying as did the Zuñi firekeeper, for the return of light: "To this end, my fathers, my children may all of you be blessed with light."[12] On the day when the light began to return, December 23, 1805, Lucy gave birth to a son, whom they named Joseph, after the name of his father.

He would grow up with a legacy of hard work and little education. In other places in the country, people lived on landed estates. They had titles and doctorates. Philosophers of religion and scholars of ancient languages studied their subjects.

"For ye see your calling . . . how that not many wise men after the flesh, not many mighty, not many noble, are called: But God hath chosen the foolish things of the world to confound the wise; and God hath chosen the weak things of the world to confound the things which are mighty." (1 Corinthians 1:26–27.)

What would we expect of a prophet's childhood? We know little about Joseph's early life except that he was "remarkably quiet [and] well-disposed," and that though not given to much reading, was inclined toward "meditation and deep study."[13]

With a living to wrest from an unyielding ground, Joseph worked with his family instead of attending much school. In his formal education, he obtained only the most rudimentary skills in reading, writing, and arithmetic. His education was of the land; his teachers were his parents and elder brothers Alvin and Hyrum, whose love and loyalty to him were unbending.

Wrote Lucy, "I suppose, from questions which are frequently asked me, that it is thought by some that I shall be likely to tell many very remarkable incidents which attended his childhood; but as nothing occurred during his early life except those trivial circumstances which are common to that state of human existence, I pass them in silence."[14]

Left: Traces of life two hundred years ago are often hidden under moss and grown over with weeds, as with this stone wall surrounding the traditional homesite where the Prophet's uncle Daniel Mack lived in the late 1700s and early 1800s. Lucy's side of the family, the Macks, were pioneers in New England, willing to take risks and work hard to take care of their families.

Above: Homesite of the Prophet's maternal grandfather, Solomon Mack (1732–1820). Solomon suffered much as a youth. He was reared by a neighborhood farmer after a tragedy in his own family, and he learned all about hard work and little else. He served in the Revolutionary War. Though crippled by a falling tree, he continued to have an active life, and he had a remarkable spiritual conversion eight years before his death.

Tunbridge, Orange County, Vermont, nestled in the verdant hills of New England. Because of the harsh topography, towns in Vermont are generally very small. Keeping accurate records has been an important role of the local governments in New England. Original entries of the births of the Smith children as well as the original entry of the marriage of Joseph Smith and Lucy Mack, dated January 24, 1796, can still be found in the town clerk's office at Tunbridge.

When Lucy and Joseph married, they had had every hope for a prosperous, comfortable life. Their families had enjoyed above average means; Lucy had been given a gift of $1,000 from her brother and his business partner; and they knew how to work hard. However, they were dogged by a series of difficult events.

Their first farm was stony and unproductive, and they were plagued by sickness. Their investment in ginseng root, which grew wild in Vermont and was in demand in China, failed due to a dishonest merchant who stole all their profits.

Young Joseph later recorded that his parents "being in indigent circumstances were obliged to labour hard for the support of a large family having nine children and . . . it required the exertions of all that were able to render any assistance."[15]

Joseph and Lucy Smith were determined to improve their fortunes. They moved from place to place striving to find their way,

to have a solid opportunity come through, to harvest a bumper crop. They lived in Randolph, Sharon, Royalton, Norwich, and Tunbridge, towns nestled close together near Vermont's Green Mountains, working toward the break they needed.

Perhaps just across the great Connecticut River at Lebanon, New Hampshire—there would be their good fortune. A little land and a small house seemed a good choice. After much effort, they saved some money and things were going better than they ever had before.

"Here we . . . doubled our diligence, in order to obtain more of this world's goods, with the view of assisting our children when they should need it; and, as is quite natural, we looked forward to the decline of life, and . . . [were] striving to procure those things which contribute much to the comfort of old age. . . . [The] children had . . . been debarred from the privilege of schools, [so] we began to make every arrangement to attend to this important duty."[16]

All the Smiths' bright prospects were dimmed with the typhoid fever epidemic of 1812 and 1813. For a year, the fever raged through their family, with first one child and then another taken sick until all were stricken. Eldest daughter Sophronia was the worst, having a severe case for over three months, recovering only by a miracle.

As the epidemic subsided, one day seven-year-old Joseph suddenly screamed out with an agonizing pain in his shoulder. The doctor claimed he could do nothing, and after two more weeks of the child's agony, the physician made closer observation and discovered a fever sore that had gathered between his breast and his shoulder.

When the doctor lanced the sore, it discharged fully a quart of matter, and the pain shot down Joseph's side into the marrow of the bone of his leg.

Joseph screamed out in pain, "Oh, father! the pain is so severe, how can I bear it!"[17]

Left: The seasons change rapidly in this weather-beaten land. Windsor County, Vermont, would greet the Smiths but once more after they faced great health trials in New Hampshire. There were few doctors, and there was limited knowledge of medicine and good health practices during Joseph Smith's boyhood. However, Dartmouth College, with its medical school, was just a few miles away.

Above: Graves in a forgotten cemetery in the woods near Tunbridge, Vermont, 1813. The deaths of David and Samuel Brewer, likely from the typhoid fever that swept through New England, remind us of the devastating nature of epidemics in those days. These brothers, ages eighteen and thirteen, passed away just months apart. They were contemporaries of Alvin and Hyrum Smith.

Evening light touches wild sumac on the Smiths' property in Lebanon, New Hampshire, circa 1812–1814. During their stay here, the Smiths sent their children to school for the first time. Hyrum was given the most education, the other children less. Joseph Smith's earthly education would never be a credential for him, for he would be tutored from the heavens.

The leg swelled until the pain was excruciating. Only one thing helped. Thirteen-year-old Hyrum, whose love for his brother was powerful, sat by his bed nearly every day and night holding the affected part of Joseph's leg in his hands and pressing it between them so that his afflicted brother might endure from minute to minute.

At the end of three weeks the surgeon was called again. He made an incision to relieve the swelling, but as soon as the leg began to heal, the pain was as violent as ever. Another operation was performed, the wound was enlarged, and, with healing, the wound again began to swell.

Finally, according to Lucy, a council of surgeons came, including one of the nation's most skilled, Dr. Nathan Smith of Dartmouth College. Their conclusion: amputate the boy's leg to save his life.

Lucy would not hear of it, and she boldly confronted them:

"You will not, you must not, take off his leg, until you try once more. I will not consent to let you enter his room until you make me this promise."[18]

She and the doctors agreed on a radical operation to cut out only the infected part of the bone. The doctors wanted Joseph bound to the bed to withstand the agonies of the operation. They also wanted him to drink some brandy to numb the pain.

He answered, "I will not touch one particle of liquor, neither will I be tied down; but I will tell you what I will do—I will have my father sit on the bed and hold me in his arms, and then I will do whatever is necessary in order to have the bone taken out."[19]

He asked his mother to leave the room, saying, "You have carried me so much, and watched over me so long, you are almost worn out. . . . Now, mother, promise me that you will not stay. . . . The Lord will help me, and I shall get through with it."[20]

The Mascoma River bordered the property of the Smiths in Lebanon, New Hampshire. Near this spot, Lucy Mack Smith came to be away from the terrible leg operation of seven-year-old Joseph. As Lucy tried to stay away from the house, surely the sounds of the water sliding over the smooth rocks were swallowed up in her thoughts and prayers for Joseph. The faith of Lucy Mack Smith would be a comfort and blessing to Joseph all the days of his life.

Above: Old home and barn, circa 1810–1820, Norwich, Vermont. Hills surrounding this small New England town are touched by the last colors of fall. Joseph and Lucy moved to this area with their seven children to make one more try at farming in this climate.

Right: Clouds swell above the Smith property in Lebanon, New Hampshire, circa 1812–1814. Lucy's faith in the Lord and her hopes of Joseph's complete recovery were undaunted. Lucy would stand by her sons all the days of their lives and outlive all of them but William.

Pages 34–35: Norwich, Vermont, would be the last place the Smiths lived in New England. Three years of crop failures here (1814–1816) convinced Joseph and Lucy to move to western New York. The Lord's ways are unsearchable. Often He does things that are not easy to understand, and yet His purposes are always fulfilled.

It can be supposed that as Lucy walked several hundred yards from the house, her heart and voice were drawn out in prayer with experienced faith for the recovery of her son. She had seen the Lord deliver her and her children from death and disease before.

Twice she entered the room upon hearing Joseph's screams of pain. Both times she was removed. Finally the ordeal was over. The operation was a miracle. Joseph's leg had been spared and his life saved, but he would be on crutches for three more years and would have a limp the rest of his life.

Lucy offered a benediction of great faith to this period in their lives: "Having passed through about a year of sickness and distress, health again returned to our family, and we most assuredly realized the blessing; and indeed, we felt to acknowledge the hand of God, more in preserving our lives through such a tremendous scene of affliction, than if we had, during this time, seen nothing but health and prosperity."[21]

Shortly after these experiences in New Hampshire, the family moved to Norwich, Vermont. Thoughts of the future and preparation for retirement were far from them as they had been reduced to nothing through their long year of misfortune in health.

The years 1814 and 1815 marked complete crop failures for the Smiths. Reports were circulating about this time that good land was available in western New York, where the soil was tilled easily and wheat was raised abundantly. Thoughts of moving came to Mr. Smith and, said he, "If [I] should meet with no better success than [I have] the two preceding years, [I will] then go to the state of New York."[22]

Carefully the seeds were planted and cultivated this third year, 1816. The Smiths watched as the seeds grew in abundance and all looked toward success. They exercised their faith, no doubt praying continually.

Their prayers were answered but not in the way they expected. As the Lord said through the prophet Isaiah, "For my thoughts are not your thoughts, neither are your ways my ways. . . . For as the heavens are higher than the earth, so are my ways higher than your ways, and my thoughts than your thoughts." (Isaiah 55:8–9.)

In the middle of June, a series of killing frosts, caused by the change in weather patterns created by the huge volcanic eruption of Mount Tambora in Indonesia the year before, raged through New England with a vengeance. Known as the year without a summer, 1816 saw all their crops destroyed. That was enough. Five generations of Smiths notwithstanding, Joseph and Lucy decided to move to a small village in the western part of New York, a village by the name of Palmyra.

After more than twenty years of marriage, the Smiths wanted only to settle down and enjoy the remainder of their lives. They had moved seven times and had tried many business and farming ventures, but now the world's goods were gone from them. The Smiths were reduced to nothing but the love they shared for each other. This love became the bond that would hold them together in the storms that were about to come.

2 LIGHTS FROM THE HEAVENS AND A VOICE FROM THE DUST

Pages 36–37: Early morning sun illuminates the dew-laden weeds and grasses in a field on the Smith property where fourteen-year-old Joseph may have walked to enter the grove to pray for guidance. Located two miles south of the village of Palmyra, New York, in Manchester Township (originally Farmington Township).

Joseph Sr. went ahead to New York to prepare a place for his family, sending Caleb Howard back with money and a team to bring them. But Howard turned out to be a scoundrel, spending all their money mid-journey on drinking and gambling, and treating the children with cruelty. Ten-year-old Joseph, still lame from his leg operation, was compelled to walk forty miles a day in snow and mud, as he said, in excruciating weariness and pain.[1]

Finally Howard dumped all their belongings and tried to steal their wagon and team. Lucy seized the horses, stopped him, and took charge for the rest of the trip, dismissing the man. She was left to pay for lodging from Utica to Palmyra with some cloth and clothing.

Reunited in Palmyra, the family had little cash, scant belongings, but a desire to obtain the good land they had heard about in western New York. Within two years, with all working together, they purchased 100 acres of heavily forested land. The first year they cleared 30 acres, erected a log house, and began planting again.

Above: Sweeping panorama of fertile fields in western New York, where, in the early 1800s, land was said to be cheap and wheat grew in abundance. Larger rolling hills in the distance are "drumlins," formed during the ice age, the same variety as the Hill Cumorah. On the right is a field next to the school where twenty-two-year-old Oliver Cowdery was teaching in 1829.

Left: Grasses just a few yards from the Sacred Grove on Smith property. Usually precipitation in this area makes irrigation unnecessary. A farmer depends on the good graces of the heavens for his harvest. Every farm boy picks a stem of grass and chews on it while pondering the things of life.

Above: Traditionally called Four Corners, in the village of Palmyra. Though these church buildings were not here when the Smiths were (the oldest was built in 1832), they represent some of the religions of the day Joseph was investigating. Spires left to right: Methodist, Episcopalian, Presbyterian, and Baptist. Canandaigua Road runs between them and heads south two miles directly to the Hill Cumorah.

Right: Crooked Creek (sometimes called Hathaway Brook or Stafford Creek) runs through the Smith property in Manchester Township. One resident says this stream has not run dry in 66 years. Farm boys love to wade in creeks and explore them from beginning to end. The source of this creek is the east side of the Hill Cumorah.

Young Joseph loved to observe the stars and their perfect order and would often ponder the order of God's creations and the disorder among the religions of humanity.[2]

It was a time and place for such questions. In 1818 a great spiritual awakening spread through rural western New York. Multitudes gathered in the fields and forest clearings to hear the great preachers, saying: "Lo, here." "Lo, there." "Here is truth. Here salvation." Many converted, but contentions erupted among them.

The war of words made Joseph concerned for the eternal welfare of his soul. He pondered these things with great seriousness, wondering what he should do. The scriptures were clear: God is the same yesterday, today, and forever. But why so much confusion?[3]

Then one day, he read in the New Testament, the Epistle of James, first chapter and fifth verse: "If any of you lack wisdom, let him ask of God, that giveth to all men liberally, and upbraideth not, and it shall be given him."

A silent witness of the First Vision. A number of trees in the Sacred Grove today were there in the days of Joseph. Majestic maple, elm, beech, oak, and other trees grace this forest. Joseph was concerned about the eternal welfare of his soul and which church he should join to help him obtain salvation. Many others had the same thing on their minds.

This was the answer—go right to the Source of all truth. Here Joseph could find the direction he needed. Here he could not be deceived. Here, if he asked with faith, nothing wavering, he would know. "This was cheering information to him," wrote Orson Pratt, "tidings that gave him great joy. It was like a light shining forth in a dark place, to guide him to the path in which he should walk. He now saw that if he inquired of God, there was not only a possibility, but a probability; yea, more, a certainty, that he should obtain a knowledge, which, of all the doctrines, was the doctrine of Christ; and, which of all the churches, was the church of Christ."[4]

On the morning of a beautiful, clear day in the spring of 1820, Joseph retired to a place in the woods on his father's farm where he knew he could be alone. This was his first attempt to pray vocally. These were familiar woods to him, friends. Looking around to be sure that he was alone, he knelt down to offer up the desires of his heart and simply ask God what he should do.

No sooner had he begun to pray than he heard the sound of footsteps of someone coming from behind him. He sprang to his feet to see who it was, but he could see no one.

He knelt again and tried to pray. "I had scarcely done so," he wrote, "when immediately I was [seized] upon by some power which entirely overcame me and had such astonishing influence over me as to bind my tongue so that I could not speak. Thick darkness gathered around me and it seemed to me . . . as if I were doomed to sudden destruction."[5]

Joseph was alone, and it seemed that nothing could free him from this power of darkness. The question about religion seemed far from him now. At the very moment when Joseph was ready to sink into despair, to be overcome by this evil power from the unseen world, "not to an imaginary ruin but to [an] actual being . . . who had such a marvelous power as I had never before felt,"[6] this young boy, fourteen years old, exerted all his remaining powers to call upon God to deliver him from this enemy.

Early morning light filters through the leaves of this hickory tree in the Sacred Grove. The canopy of tall trees invited Joseph and others of his family to come to the forest on occasion for secret prayer. The vision that Joseph would receive would change the course of religious history and show to the world that God did speak again from the heavens.

At this moment of great alarm, "I saw a pillar of light exactly over my head above the brightness of the sun, which descended gradually until it fell upon me. It no sooner appeared than I found myself delivered from the enemy which held me bound."[7]

"I was enwrapped in a heavenly vision and saw two glorious personages . . . who exactly resembled each other in features and likeness, surrounded with a brilliant light which eclipsed the sun at noon day."[8]

"One of them spake unto me calling me by name and said (pointing to the other) 'This is my beloved Son, Hear him.'"[9] "He spake unto me saying, 'Joseph, my son, thy sins are forgiven thee. Go thy way, walk in my statutes and keep my commandments. Behold, I am the Lord of glory. I was crucified for the world that all those who believe on my name may have eternal life.'"[10]

"My object in going to enquire of the Lord," Joseph wrote, "was to know which of all the sects was right, that I might know which to join. . . . I asked the personages who stood above me in the light, which of all the sects was right . . . and which I should join. I was answered that I must join none of them, for they were all wrong."[11] "The world lieth in sin at this time and none doeth good, no not one. They have turned aside from the gospel and keep not my commandments."[12] The Lord also said "that all their Creeds were an abomination in his sight, that those professors were all corrupt, that 'they draw near to me with their lips but their hearts are far from me, They teach for doctrines the commandments of men, having a form of Godliness but they deny the power thereof.' He again forbade me to join with any of them and many other things did he say unto me which I cannot write at this time."[13] "[I was given] a promise that the fullness of the Gospel should at some future time be made known unto me."[14]

"When the light had departed I had no strength, but soon recovering in some degree, I went home. . . . I leaned up to the fire piece. Mother enquired what the matter was. I replied, 'Never mind, all is well. I am well enough off.'"[15] "My soul was filled with love and for many days I could rejoice with great joy and the Lord was with me."[16] God had pierced the heavens and spoken to man once more. It was the beginning of the Dispensation of the Fullness of Times.

Light dances through the tops of the trees and fills the grove with warmth and an invitation for Joseph and others to seek the heavens in solemn prayer and meditation. Somewhere near this place Joseph witnessed the grand theophany of the last days. God was opening a new dispensation of the gospel, and Joseph Smith was called to be the mighty Prophet of the Restoration.

What did young Joseph feel as he walked back out of this now sacred grove of trees? God the Eternal Father and His Son Jesus Christ did answer his humble prayer! What rapture must truly have filled his bosom!

Days passed, and Joseph took the opportunity to share his experience with one of the ministers from whom he had earlier sought direction: "I was greatly surprised at his behaviour, he treated my communication not only lightly but with great contempt, saying it was all of the Devil, that there was no such thing as visions or revelations in these days, that all such things had ceased with the apostles and that there never would be any more of them. I soon found . . . that my telling the story had excited a great deal of prejudice against me among professors of religion and was the cause of great persecution which continued to increase . . . and this was common among all the sects: all united to persecute me."[17]

"It caused me serious reflection then, and often has since, how very strange it was that an obscure boy, of a little over fourteen years of age, and one, too, who was doomed to the necessity of obtaining a scanty maintenance by his daily labor, should be thought a character of sufficient importance to attract the attention of the great ones of the most popular sects of the day, and in a manner to create in them a spirit of the most bitter persecution and reviling. . . .

"It was nevertheless a fact that I had beheld a vision. . . .

"I had actually seen a light, and in the midst of that light I saw two Personages, and they did in reality speak to me; and though I was hated and persecuted for saying that I had seen a vision, yet it was true; and while they were persecuting me, reviling me, and speaking all manner of evil against me falsely for so saying, I was led to say in my heart: Why persecute me for telling the truth? I have actually seen a vision; and who am I that I can withstand God, or why does the world think to make me deny what I have actually seen? For I had seen a vision; I knew it, and I knew that God knew it, and I could not deny it, neither dared I do it; at least I knew that by so doing I would offend God, and come under condemnation."[18]

Pages 46–47: Sentinels and friends, the trees stood silently as Joseph walked out of the grove. What he learned on that beautiful spring day in 1820 would defy all the religions of the world. This fourteen-year-old boy was to be an instrument in the hands of God to bring about the "restitution of all things" spoken of by the holy prophets since the world began. (Acts 3:21.)

Above: Joseph, with his brothers and father, used to work in this field tilling and taming the land. It was hard work to clear virgin, native forest in Western New York with more than 100 large trees to the acre. But hard work also brought physical growth and renewed strength to the boy prophet. Joseph was much like other boys, jovial and playful, with a "native cheery temperament." (Joseph Smith–History 1:28.)

The process of clearing land for cultivation was an arduous one. The forest was dense. Some of the ancient trees the Smiths were clearing had been fifty years old when Christopher Columbus came to America. Many had trunks whose diameter ranged from two to four feet across, while some of the elms likely reached the massive proportions of nine to ten feet.

Felling hardwood trees was good training for the young boy prophet. He began to gain strength in his left leg again. His arms developed, and his quickness and agility grew along with his natural build so that Joseph became known for his physical strength and skill. His abilities in wrestling, stick-pulling, and "jumping the mark" would be unsurpassed by any of his contemporaries. This physical prowess would later prove useful to him in dealing with mobs and detractors.

Even before the First Vision, an attempt was made on Joseph's life. Lucy recorded: "He was out one evening on an errand, and, on

Modern path to the Sacred Grove in fall. Tens of thousands of people now come each year from all parts of the world to visit this place and ponder the great events that occurred here. Three and a half years had passed since the First Vision, and now seventeen-year-old Joseph wanted to know his state and standing before the Lord.

returning home, as he was passing through the dooryard, a gun was fired across his pathway with the evident intention of shooting him. He sprang to the door much frightened. We immediately went in search of the assassin, but could find no trace of him that evening. The next morning we found his tracks under a wagon where he lay when he fired, and the following day we found the balls which were discharged from the gun, lodged in the head and neck of a cow that was standing opposite the wagon in a dark corner."[19]

Joseph did not receive the fulness of the mantle of this calling as a prophet all at once but received experience for experience, grace for grace, lesson for lesson, truth for truth. The pattern was shown by the Savior, for, as Paul wrote, "Though he were a Son, yet learned he obedience by the things which he suffered." (Hebrews 5:8.) The hard tutoring continued in the world's school, but the heavens were now to be opened again.

Joseph continued pursuing the common avocations of life until the late evening of September 21, 1823, when Joseph betook himself to prayer and supplication to "Almighty God for forgiveness of all my sins . . . and also for a manifestation to me that I might know of my state and standing before him. For I had full confidence in obtaining a divine manifestation as I had previously had one.

"While I was thus in the act of calling upon God, I discovered a light appearing in the room which continued to increase . . . when immediately a personage appeared at my bedside standing in the air for his feet did not touch the floor.

"He had on a loose robe of most exquisite whiteness. It was a whiteness beyond anything earthly I had ever seen, nor do I believe that any earthly thing could be made to appear so exceedingly white and brilliant. . . . Not only was his robe exceedingly white but his whole person was glorious beyond description, and his countenance truly like lightning. The room was exceedingly light, but not so very bright as immediately around his person. When I first looked upon him I was afraid, but the fear soon left me.

"He called me by name and said unto me that he was a messenger sent from the presence of God . . . and that his name was Moroni. That God had a work for me to do, and that my name should be had for good and evil among all nations kindreds and tongues. . . .

"He said there was a book deposited written upon gold plates, giving an account of the former inhabitants of this continent and the source from whence they sprang. He also said that the fullness of the everlasting Gospel was contained in it as delivered by the Saviour to the ancient inhabitants. . . . While he was conversing with me about the plates the vision was opened to my mind that I could see the place where the plates were deposited and that so clearly and distinctly that I knew the place again when I visited it. . . . He informed me of great judgements which were coming upon the earth, with great desolations by famine, sword, and pestilence . . . [after he ascended] I lay overwhelmed in astonishment at what I had both seen and heard."[20]

Thus began a series of powerful tutoring sessions for the seventeen-year-old boy Joseph. Moroni came to him two more times that night and twice the following day. Among many other instructions, Joseph was commanded to tell his father of the visits.

Standing in the fields on this day, the beginning of the harvest season, Joseph rehearsed to his father all that had transpired the night before. His father replied in great faith that "it was of God"[21] and that he should go and do as commanded by the messenger.

Joseph wrote: "I left the field and went to the place where the messenger had told me the plates were deposited [about two miles from his home], and owing to the distinctness of the vision which I had had concerning it, I knew the place the instant that I arrived there. Under a stone of considerable size, lay the plates deposited in a stone box. . . . I made an attempt to take them out but was forbidden by the messenger and was . . . informed that the time for bringing them forth had not yet arrived, neither would until four years from that time, but he told me that I should come to that place precisely in one year from that time, and that he would there meet with me, and I should continue to do so until the time should come for obtaining the plates."[22]

Joseph's mother said of this period: "From this time forth, Joseph continued to receive instructions from the Lord, and we continued to get the children together every evening for the purpose of listening while he gave us a relation of the same. I presume our family presented an aspect as singular as any that ever lived upon the face of the earth—all seated in a circle, father, mother, sons and daughters, and giving the most profound attention to a boy, eighteen years of age, who had never read the Bible through in his life. . . .

"Joseph would occasionally give us some of the most amusing recitals that could be imagined. He would describe the ancient inhabitants of this continent, their dress, mode of traveling, and the animals upon which they rode; their cities, their buildings, with every particular; their mode of warfare; and also their religious worship. This he would do with as much ease, seemingly, as if he had spent his whole life among them."[23]

Pages 50–51: Looking toward the west side of the Hill Cumorah in fall. This is the tallest of any of the "drumlin" hills in the area. Over 200,000 trees have been planted on the Hill Cumorah in recent times. In Joseph's day there were only some small stands of timber on the hill. The approach to the west side of the hill may have looked similar to this in his day. The ancient record was found on this side of the hill not far from the top.

Right: Statue of the ancient Nephite Prophet Moroni (circa A.D. 350–421) high atop the Hill Cumorah, depicting "another angel [flying] in the midst of heaven, having the everlasting gospel to preach unto them that dwell on the earth, and to every nation, and kindred, and tongue, and people." (Revelation 14:6.) This angel came to Joseph at least twenty-two times in seven years.

Frame house of the Smiths in Manchester Township, Ontario County, New York. Eldest son Alvin began building this house in 1822 for his parents. At that time the Smiths had nine children, all at home, and they lived in a small cabin at the north end of their 100 acres. "I remember well the pangs of sorrow that swelled my . . . tender heart when [Alvin] died," Joseph wrote. "He was the oldest and noblest of my father's family. He was one of the noblest of the sons of men."[24]

Above: Western light bathes this upstairs bedroom in the Smith frame house. Sensing his approaching death, Alvin called Joseph to his bedside. "I want you to be a good boy, and do everything that lies in your power to obtain the Record,"[25] he said to Joseph. Alvin died at 24 years and nine months of age.

Right: West-facing porch of the Smith frame home looking south. Four revelations canonized in the Doctrine and Covenants were received on the Smith property. Alvin's workmanship and careful hand is evident in many parts of the house. Eighteen years later, after another of his brothers had been taken in death, Joseph said, "It has been hard for me to live on earth and see these young men, upon whom we have leaned for support and comfort, taken from us in the midst of their youth."[26]

The carefully planed rails and fitted beams, the fine workmanship on moldings and doors—everything about the Smith family home stands today, but its builder, Joseph's eldest and adored brother Alvin, did not live to see it completed, a house he had arranged for his parents' comfort in their aging years. Things stand long after their builders have perished.

In November 1823, just eight weeks after Moroni's visit, Alvin, in his mid twenties, was taken seriously ill with something his mother called "bilious colic."[27] He was administered a large dose of calomel by an incompetent doctor. The medicine lodged in his stomach, and he died four days later.

The effect of this untimely death was great on the Smiths. Whenever Joseph spoke of the Record, it would immediately bring Alvin to their minds, and when they looked to his place at the table, Lucy wrote, "and realized that he was gone from it, to return no more in this life, we all with one accord wept over our irretrievable loss."[28]

Interest and rumors followed Joseph Smith because he had found gold plates. Probably in the spirit of the rumors, Josiah Stowell hired Joseph at age nineteen to come to work for him to help find an old Spanish silver mine near Harmony, Pennsylvania. After a few weeks with no success, Stowell gave him other work.

Still, Joseph found something more valuable to him while boarding at the home of Isaac and Elizabeth Hale, also of Harmony. There he met Emma Hale, their well-educated, schoolteacher daughter. Emma was dark haired, refined, and polished. Joseph was a farm boy, rough and unfinished. Isaac Hale was much against their developing courtship. However, Joseph and Emma grew in love.

Joseph told his parents, "I have been very lonely ever since Alvin died and I have concluded to get married, and if you have no objections to my uniting myself . . . with Miss Emma Hale, she would be my choice in preference to any other woman I have ever seen."[29]

Left: Surrounding countryside south of the Smith property in Manchester Township. Joseph, his father, and his brothers would often hire out their labor to neighbors. They would dig wells, plow fields, remove trees, build homes, and do whatever other jobs were available. It was a struggle to gather the full $100 needed for the payment on their property each year.

Above: Part of the Joseph Knight Sr. farm in Colesville (now Ninevah), New York. The first branch of the Church was formed here. At age twenty, Joseph came to work for the Knights doing farm work and likely helping in their sawmill. Newell Knight became very close to Joseph, and all of the family loved him. The Knights lent financial support for the translation of the Book of Mormon and other timely aid. Joseph and Emma were married near here in South Bainbridge, New York, January 18, 1827.

The glow of fall enwraps this sacred place, the Hill Cumorah. During one of Joseph's visits to the hill, the Angel Moroni showed him a vision of the hosts of hell and the kingdom of the devil, and then, in contrast, showed him the glory and majesty of the kingdom of heaven. Lucy wrote, "The impression [made on this occasion] was always vivid in his memory until the very end of his days . . . [and] ever afterwards he was willing to keep the commandments of God."[30] On September 22, 1827, Joseph was entrusted with the ancient record. The word Cumorah *may come from two Hebrew roots meaning "to gather together light or knowledge."[31]*

Joseph and Emma probably lived in this room in the Smith frame house in Manchester for the first few months of their marriage. This would be the beginning of at least fifteen homes they would live in during the next seventeen years. Lucy Mack Smith and Emma Hale Smith formed a friendship here that would never be broken.

A special timing, set by the Lord, was attached to the coming forth of these ancient records from the dust. Moroni had been the one who buried them in the Hill Cumorah in A.D. 421, the last scribe of a fallen people. All the prophets before him who had recorded their testimonies on the plates had known they were for another people besides themselves—a people of the latter days—and their message was urgent.

As Moroni wrote to us on these records during his lifetime, "Behold, I speak unto you as if ye were present, and yet ye are not. But behold, Jesus Christ hath shown you unto me, and I know your doing." (Mormon 8:35.) The message of these plates held a witness from the ancient world to the modern one that Jesus is the Christ, the Redeemer of the world, that He had visited His people on the American continent and taught His gospel and given them His authority. And the plates held a solemn warning about what happens to an entire civilization who rejects Him.

The living room in the Smith frame house in Manchester. Mobs were constantly on the prowl to steal the gold plates from Joseph. He had to keep them secluded in different places, once in an old birch log, once in the loft of the cooper's shop on their farm, and once under the hearth of the fireplace in this room. The constant attempts of the mob to obtain the plates add ironic evidence and testimony of their existence.

So on September 22, 1827, at last the time had come for the plates to come forth and be translated by the gift and power of God. Joseph's mother remembers, "About twelve o'clock [at night], Joseph came to me and asked if I had a chest with a lock and key. I knew in an instant what he wanted it for."[32]

In the dark of the night, Joseph and Emma drove in a borrowed wagon to the hill where Joseph was allowed to take the plates. With them, attached to a breastplate, was a Urim and Thummim, two ancient stones through which records could be translated and revelation given.

Moroni, who understood the importance of these records, warned Joseph, "Now you have got the Record into your own hands, and you are but a man, therefore you will have to be watchful and faithful to your trust, or you will be overpowered by wicked men; for they will lay every plan and scheme that is possible to get it away from you."[33]

63

Lake cobblestone home (circa 1850) built on the original foundation of Martin Harris's home in Palmyra, New York. Martin was scribe for Joseph, gave aid to Joseph and Emma, became one of the special witnesses of the Book of Mormon, mortgaged his farm to finance the printing of the Book of Mormon, and was ever true to his testimony. His trip to see Professor Anthon fulfilled a prophecy of Isaiah: "The vision of all is become unto you as the words of a book that is sealed, which men deliver to one that is learned, saying, Read this, I pray thee: and he saith, I cannot; for it is sealed: and the book is delivered to him that is not learned, saying, Read this, I pray thee: and he saith, I am not learned." (Isaiah 29:11–12.)

As Moroni had warned, rumors circulated about the gold plates, and mobs formed to steal them from Joseph. No place was secure for long in the face of the constant threats and violence.

Now, when they needed it most, Joseph and Emma found a welcome friend in one of the most respectable farmers in Palmyra, Martin Harris, who helped liquidate their debts and gave them fifty dollars to move to Emma's parents' home in Harmony. The couple made the 110-mile journey with Emma being pregnant with their first child, and they arrived in the winter cold of December.

Martin soon came and obtained from Joseph a copy of some of the ancient characters from the plates, with a translation, and took them to Professor Charles Anthon of Columbia College in New York City. Anthon, a scholar of ancient languages, studied the characters and said that the translation was the most correct he had ever seen. He signed a paper stating this to the people of Palmyra. But upon hearing from Martin about the source of the plates, he took the certificate back and tore it to pieces, saying that there was no such thing as ministering of angels and that if Martin would bring him the plates he would translate them. Martin said that part of the plates were sealed and that he was forbidden to see them. Anthon replied, "I cannot read a sealed book."[34]

Martin came back to Harmony and assisted Joseph as scribe for nearly nine weeks. By June 14, 1828, they had completed enough of the work to fill 116 pages of manuscript paper.

Throughout the process, Martin had begged Joseph to let him take the manuscript to Palmyra to show his wife and others so he could retain his good reputation. Though Martin pled with Joseph to ask the Lord for permission, the Lord twice said no. Martin continued to plead. Finally, he was allowed to take the manuscript under oath and covenant to show it only to those whom he had promised.

Only hours after Martin left, the world turned dark for Joseph. Emma gave birth to their first son, who was snatched from her arms by the hand of death, and, in grief and illness, she seemed on the edge of death herself. For two weeks, Joseph slept not an hour of undisturbed quiet, and, on the third week, as Emma was recovering, another anxiety forced itself upon him. Where was Martin?

Joseph went to Palmyra and sent for Martin. After several hours he came, head bowed and heart low. Silently, Martin sat down at the table, crying out in deep anguish, "Oh, I have lost my soul!" "Martin, have you lost that manuscript? Have you broken your oath?" "Yes; it is gone, and I know not where." Joseph cried out, "All is lost! all is lost! What shall I do? . . . I should have been satisfied with the first answer I received from the Lord. . . . Of what rebuke am I not worthy from the angel of the Most High?"[35] He wept and groaned and walked the floor continually. He could not be comforted as he understood so well the consequences of disobedience.

"The next morning, he set out for home. We parted with heavy hearts," recorded his mother, "for it now appeared that all which we had so fondly anticipated, and which had been the source of so much secret gratification, had in a moment fled, and fled forever."[36]

Stone marking the grave of the infant son of Joseph and Emma in Harmony Township, Susquehanna County, Pennsylvania. As happy and anxious as any young couple, Joseph and Emma looked forward to the birth of their first child together. Disappointment was great as the baby boy was taken from them. Their next two children would be taken in death as well. Though no name is shown on the gravestone, the family Bible suggests that they named this first son Alvin.

Above: Detail of sculpture by Avard Fairbanks in Harmony, Pennsylvania, depicting the hand of John the Baptist conferring the Priesthood of Aaron upon the head of Joseph Smith. Joseph recorded, "Our minds being now enlightened, we began to have the Scriptures laid open to our understandings . . . in a manner which we never could attain to previously, nor ever before had thought of."[37]

Right: Woods on original 13 1/2 acres of property of Joseph and Emma in Harmony, Pennsylvania. Joseph went to work this land to see to the needs of the family, but he found it impossible to work and translate. Then timely aid arrived from Joseph Knight Sr. (he lived thirty miles from here) who gave them a barrel of mackerel, about ten bushels of grain, six bushels of potatoes, and some lined paper for writing. The provisions lasted them to the end of the translation.

Joseph was but a man, and he had succumbed to the influences and pressures of man. "For, behold," the Lord told him, "you should not have feared man more than God. . . . You should have been faithful; and he would have extended his arm and supported you against all the fiery darts of the adversary; and he would have been with you in every time of trouble." (D&C 3:7–8.)

Upon Joseph's return to Harmony, Moroni took the Urim and Thummim and the privilege to translate from him, and these gifts were not returned for several months. When returned, a promise was given that a scribe would be sent to help Joseph in the work. He was told not to retranslate the part he had already done, as the manuscript had fallen into evil hands who wanted to prove the work a fraud. Another part of the plates, he was told, would cover this same period, and the work of these evil men would be foiled.

Back in Manchester, the Smiths were boarding a young schoolteacher, Oliver Cowdery, with whom they shared the marvelous story of their son Joseph. Oliver retired to a secret place to ask the Lord if what he had heard was true, and the Lord spoke peace to his mind about the matter. As the Lord later told him, "What greater witness can you have than from God?" (D&C 6:23.)

Oliver became consumed with the desire to write for Joseph, so he traveled to Harmony, arriving Sunday, April 5, 1829, to meet the Prophet for the first time. On Tuesday the great work of translation began, Joseph peering at the plates through the Urim and Thummim, Oliver writing what Joseph dictated.

"These were days never to be forgotten—to sit under the sound of a voice dictated by the inspiration of heaven awakened the utmost gratitude of this bosom!" recounted Oliver. "Day after day I continued, uninterrupted, to write from his mouth, as he translated . . . the history, or record, called 'the book of Mormon.'"[38]

Thirty-eight days into the translation, Joseph and Oliver were deep in discussion about the true mode and authority of baptism. They retired to the woods to ask for guidance from God. "The Lord, who is rich in mercy, and ever willing to answer the consistent prayer of the humble . . . condescended to manifest to us his will,"[39] wrote Oliver.

Oliver recorded: "On a sudden, as from the midst of eternity . . . the veil was parted and the angel of God came down clothed with glory. . . . What Joy! what wonder! what amazement! . . . 'I am thy fellow servant.'" the angel said.[40] "[He] said that his name was John, the same that is called John the Baptist in the New Testament, and that he acted under the direction of Peter, James and John who held the keys of the Priesthood of Melchizedek, which Priesthood he said would in due time be conferred on us."[41]

John laid his hands upon Joseph and Oliver and ordained them, saying: "Upon you my fellow servants, in the name of Messiah I confer the Priesthood of Aaron, which holds the keys of the ministering of angels, and of the gospel of repentance, and of baptism by immersion for the remission of sins." (D&C 13.)

Upon commandment, the two then baptized each other by immersion in the Susquehanna River. Joseph baptized Oliver, and then Oliver baptized Joseph. Upon coming up out of the water, each was filled with the spirit of prophecy and of the Holy Ghost. Now the true authority and keys of baptism were restored to the earth!

"I shall not attempt to paint to you," Oliver recalled, "the feelings of this heart, nor the majestic beauty and glory which surrounded us on this occasion; but . . . earth, nor men, with the eloquence of time cannot begin to clothe language in as interesting and sublime a manner as this holy personage."[42]

As God's promises are always fulfilled, just weeks later another glorious visitation occurred: Peter, James, and John, apostles of Jesus Christ, appeared and conferred upon them the Melchizedek Priesthood and gave unto them the keys of the apostleship, keys no mortal had held for centuries.

As light began to be poured out upon the translator and the scribe, so did opposition grow. Interruptions became frequent, and the work began to slow. They needed a quieter place to continue the translation. David Whitmer, a friend of Oliver's, was informed of their plight, and David's parents, Peter and Mary, responded by inviting Oliver, Joseph, and Emma to come to live with them in Fayette, New York.

Pages 68–69: Near here Joseph Smith and Oliver Cowdery received the Aaronic Priesthood under the hands of John the Baptist. Here also, in the Susquehanna River, were the first baptisms performed with true authority in these last days. Much of the translation of the Book of Mormon was completed in the home located about two hundred yards from here (no longer standing). Fifteen canonized revelations were received at or near the residence.

Above: A depiction of the translation area in the upper bedroom of the Whitmer farmhouse. The words were given to Joseph through the ancient Urim and Thummim and by the Spirit. The Lord gave His own witness about Joseph in a revelation, saying, "He has translated the book, even that part which I have commanded him, and as your Lord and your God liveth, it is true." (D&C 17:6.)

"When I arrived at Harmony," David Whitmer recorded, "Joseph and Oliver were coming toward me, and met me some distance from the house. Oliver told me that Joseph had informed him when I started from home, where I had stopped the first night, how I read the sign at the tavern, where I stopped the next night, etc., and that I would be there that day before dinner . . . all at which I was greatly astonished."[43] David brought them the ninety-five miles back to Fayette.

Joseph was much relieved to now be surrounded by new friends and people genuinely interested in the work. John Whitmer, brother of David, especially offered his services as scribe. The work began to move forward with great speed.

"The larger part of this labor was done in my presence and where I could see and know what was being done," Emma stated. "During no part of it did Joseph Smith have any [manuscript] or book of any kind from which to read or dictate except the metalic plates which I knew he had. . . . Joseph Smith could neither write nor dictate a coherent and well-worded letter, let alone dictate a book like the Book of Mormon. . . . The Book of Mormon is of divine authenticity—I have not the slightest doubt of it . . . when acting as his scribe, [Joseph] would dictate to me hour after hour; and when returning after meals, or after interruptions, he would at once begin where he had left off, without either seeing the manuscript or having any portion of it read to him. . . . It would have been improbable that a learned man could do this; and, for one so ignorant and unlearned as he was, it was simply impossible."[44]

"I testify to the world," wrote David Whitmer, "that I am an eye-witness to the translation of the greater part of the Book of Mormon. . . . No man could read it [the ancient characters], but God gave to an unlearned boy the gift to translate. . . . Joseph would read . . . the English to Oliver Cowdery, who was his principal scribe. . . . Thus the Book of Mormon was translated by the gift and power of God, and not by any power of man."[45]

Oliver added, "I wrote with my own pen the entire book of Mormon (save a few pages) as it fell from the lips of the Prophet as he translated it by the gift and power of God by means of the Urim and Thummim. . . . That book is true."[46]

Reconstruction of the Peter Whitmer Sr. farmhouse in Fayette, Seneca County, New York, where Joseph and Emma and Oliver were invited to stay and complete the translation of the sacred record. This invitation was timely because of threatened mob actions in Harmony. The people in Fayette were generally friendly and very interested in the work and in Joseph Smith.

"My father and mother had a large family... the addition to it... of Joseph, his wife Emma and Oliver very greatly increased the toil and anxiety of my mother,"47 recorded David Whitmer.

One day in June 1829, Mary was going out to milk the cows and to her great surprise was met by the Angel Moroni. He said to her, "You have been very faithful and diligent in your labors, but you are tired . . . it is proper therefore that you should receive a witness that your faith may be strengthened."48 Thereupon, the messenger showed Mary the plates, turning them over leaf by leaf, that she might know that the work was true. He promised her that if she endured in faith to the end, her reward would be sure.

Although she had never complained, she had sometimes felt that her labors were too much. This gift from the heavens completely removed all such feelings and buoyed her up for the load that was placed upon her. She was a strong believer in the Book of Mormon to the day of her death.

Left: South side of the Peter Whitmer Sr. cabin in Fayette, looking west. This home became a gathering place for believers, including Orrin Porter Rockwell, who, as a four-year-old in Manchester, befriended Joseph and was ever true to him. Elizabeth Ann Whitmer, a daughter, lived in this home and later married Oliver Cowdery. They had six children, but only one lived to maturity. Mary Whitmer received her special witness near this place in June 1829.

Above: Kitchen area in the restored Whitmer farmhouse with period furnishings. Mary Whitmer worked steadily over the fires here to keep her family and guests fed. Wherever the Prophet lived, many people came to see and meet with him. A common courtesy of the day was to feed all who came to visit. The toil and labor became very great for Mary.

Above: Dry weeds on the Whitmer property at Fayette, New York. "During this time," said Newel Knight, "we had much of the power of God manifested among us and it was wonderful to witness the wisdom that Joseph displayed . . . for truly God gave unto him great wisdom and power."[49] *Joseph desired that all might know for themselves and have their own testimony of the truthfulness of the work by the power of the Holy Ghost.*

Right: Somewhere near this place on the Whitmer property, Oliver Cowdery, David Whitmer, and Martin Harris received a special witness of the truthfulness of the Book of Mormon. Because the testimony of these three men was published with the Book of Mormon, thousands questioned them all their lives about the truthfulness of their statements. Oliver lived to be 44, David Whitmer, 83, and Martin Harris, 92, and none of them ever denied his witness.

The Apostle Paul taught that "in the mouth of two or three witnesses shall every word be established." (2 Corinthians 13:1.) So it was with the ancient record just translated, the Book of Mormon. Others besides Joseph were to be allowed to see the gold plates. Oliver Cowdery, David Whitmer, and Martin Harris, all of whom had had much to do with the record, desired with all their hearts to be those special witnesses with Joseph.

Accordingly, the four of them went into a nearby grove and began offering up their prayers to God that He would give them a view of the ancient record and a sure witness of the same. For some time they prayed with great fervency, but to no avail. Martin Harris felt himself unworthy and left the other three.

They began to pray again. Later they recorded, "We beheld a light above us in the air of exceeding brightness, and behold, an angel stood before us; in his hands he held the plates . . . he turned over the leaves one by one, so that we could see them, and discern the engravings thereon distinctly . . . immediately afterwards we heard a voice from out of the bright light above us, saying 'These plates have been revealed by the power of God, and . . . have been translated by the power of God; the translation of them which you have seen is correct, and I command you to bear record of what you now see and hear.'"[50]

After this manifestation, Joseph went a considerable distance and found Martin fervently engaged in prayer. He had not yet prevailed with the Lord and desired Joseph to join him. Ultimately, the same vision and witness was given to him. "'Tis enough, 'tis enough; mine eyes have beheld," he said. Then "jumping up he shouted, Hosanna, blessing God; and otherwise rejoiced exceedingly."[51]

Upon returning to the Whitmer home, Joseph threw himself down by his parents and said, "You do not know how happy I am: the Lord has now caused the plates to be shown to three more besides myself. They have seen an angel, who has testified to them, and they will have to bear witness to the truth of what I have said, for now they know for themselves, that I do not go about to deceive the people, and I feel as if I was relieved of a burden which was almost too heavy for me to bear, and it rejoices my soul, that I am not any longer to be entirely alone in the world."[52]

Now came the great task of publishing the manuscript as a book. For perspective, consider that large print jobs of that day were 2,000 copies of a two- to three-page pamphlet or 1,000 copies of a book.

Joseph and Oliver searched for a printer who would take on the mammoth order they had in mind—5,000 copies of a 590-page book! Two printers in nearby Rochester, New York, were approached, but one said he did not believe in the work because an angel had been involved; the other wanted an exorbitant price.

Finally, Egbert B. Grandin, age twenty-three, printer of Palmyra's local newspaper the *Wayne Sentinel,* agreed to take on the job for $3,000. Joseph turned for money to the place he had turned before: Martin Harris secured the contract with a mortgage and bond note on his farm with the debt to be paid in eighteen months. The note was signed in August 1829.

Hyrum Smith, who resided near Palmyra, was overseer for the project. For several months he made almost daily trips to the printer's shop. Because the original manuscript had very little punctuation or capitalization, John H. Gilbert, typesetter, was allowed to punctuate the book. A printer's manuscript (a copy of the original) was handwritten by Oliver Cowdery and delivered to the printer twenty-four pages at a time for security reasons. The massive project proceeded on schedule.

Five months into the printing, Palmyra was alive with talk about the so-called "gold Bible." The people of the village "held a mass meeting and passed a resolution pledging themselves not to purchase the Book of Mormon when published, and to use their influence to prevent others from purchasing it. This had the effect of causing Mr. Grandin to suspend printing until he could obtain renewed assurance of receiving the amount agreed upon for the printing the edition of five thousand."[53] It was only by persuasion from Joseph and Martin assuring him of payment that he finally continued.

On March 26, 1830, the book went on sale at the Palmyra Book Store to a cold reception. Sales could not pay the printing costs. One year and two weeks later, Martin Harris sold his farm to pay the printer's debt.

Left: On the third floor of this building in Palmyra, Wayne County, New York, the Book of Mormon was first printed and published. Nearly 400,000 eight-page "signatures" were bound on the second floor of the Grandin Building in the bindery. On the first floor, the book was put on sale at the Palmyra Bookstore, owned by Mr. Grandin. Few copies were purchased from this store.

Above: Western light touches apples growing in an orchard on the farm of Peter Whitmer Sr. Early records indicate that a majority of settlers had orchards. This fruit stands as a symbol of the sweetness of the gospel of Jesus Christ, a reminder of the fruit of the tree of life, "which [is] desirable above all other fruit" (1 Nephi 8:15) and is freely offered by the Lord.

The day had arrived. By revelation Joseph was told to officially organize the Church according to the laws of the land. This was "the beginning of the rising up and the coming forth of my church out of the wilderness—clear as the moon, and fair as the sun, and terrible as an army with banners." (D&C 5:14.)

The Church was organized the 6th day of April, 1830, commemorating the birth date of the Savior Jesus Christ, in the home of Peter and Mary Whitmer. New York law required at least three and no more than nine members to found a religious organization.[54] Six were chosen among the fifty or so present: Joseph Smith Jr., Oliver Cowdery, David Whitmer, Hyrum Smith, Samuel H. Smith, and Peter Whitmer Jr.

Joseph Smith and Oliver Cowdery were accepted and sustained as the first elders of the newly formed church. The holy sacrament was then instituted and passed to all who were present. Members were confirmed by the laying on of hands, and the Holy Ghost was poured out in a miraculous manner. Many prophesied, spiritual gifts were poured out upon them, and some declared that the heavens were opened unto them and they saw Jesus Christ sitting on the right hand of God.

The ancient church established by Jesus Christ, long lost to apostasy, was now restored, ready to be sent to the world. And indeed, the "field [was] white already to harvest . . . he that thrusteth in his sickle with his might, the same layeth up in store that he perisheth not, but bringeth salvation to his soul." (D&C 4:4.)

Samuel Smith, younger brother of Joseph, was among the first missionaries of the Church after its organization, traveling without purse or scrip to the surrounding communities. His mission was to sell copies of the Book of Mormon and preach the restored gospel of Jesus Christ.

Seeking shelter at night under trees or in barns, relying on the hospitality of strangers for food, Samuel worked his way through the countryside with limited success. Finally, however, he found one circuit preacher, John Greene, who agreed to retain the book to sell to any interested parties he found.

Pages 78–79: In this 20-by-20-foot room (reconstruction) of the Whitmer farmhouse, the Church was organized on April 6, 1830. Great joy was manifest in the hearts of all those present. In or near this home, twenty revelations were received by the Prophet Joseph; these were later canonized.

Above: The Book of Mormon and the Bible (in the window of the Whitmer farmhouse) have become one in testifying to the world that Jesus is the Christ. The Book of Mormon also stands as a witness, "Proving . . . that God does inspire men and call them to his holy work in this age and generation . . . ; thereby showing that he is the same God yesterday, today, and forever." (D&C 20:11–12.)

Right: The work of the Lord was sent forth from this place, the Whitmer farmhouse, to the surrounding communities and then to all the world. The ancient Church had been restored with all keys, gifts, and power.

Samuel Smith returned five times to retrieve the book from the Greenes, and on the last visit, John's wife, Rhoda, confessed she had secretly read the book and knew it was true. The Spirit told Samuel to leave that book with her.

About this same time, Rhoda's brother, Phineas H. Young, obtained a book from Samuel. Phineas shared it with his brother, Brigham, and also with his sister, Fanny Young Murray. Fanny shared it with her daughter, Vilate Kimball, who in turn shared it with her husband, Heber C. Kimball. John Greene also read it. After thorough study of the book, Brigham Young said, "I knew it was true, as well as I knew that I could see with my eyes."[55]

From this one effort, numerous people were converted and came into the Church, one of whom would later succeed Joseph at his death and lead the Church for thirty-three years. "And thus we see that by small means the Lord can bring about great things." (1 Nephi 16:29.)

Early morning light on Seneca Lake, where some of the first baptisms were performed. Joseph Smith's parents attended the meeting to organize the Church and were baptized shortly after, to his great joy and happiness. Parley Pratt called this lake "a beautiful and transparent sheet of water in Western New York."[56] Little did young Parley know that in less than twenty-seven years he would fall a martyr to assassins' bullets while serving a mission to preach the gospel he now embraced.

I said to my father one day when we were laboring together in the forest: 'Father, how is it there is so manifest a difference between the ancient and modern disciples of Jesus Christ and their doctrines?'"[57]

This was the question of young Parley P. Pratt. Like him, men and women everywhere were wondering where they could find the ancient gospel preached by Jesus Christ.

The work of restoration and preaching the gospel to the world was not to be Joseph's alone. Many had been prepared by the Spirit of the Lord to receive that restoration and to carry out the work. Years after he had asked that question, Parley P. Pratt left his comfortable home and lovely surroundings in Ohio on a quest to seek the authority of the ancients and the apostolic blessings.

He and his wife purchased passage all the way from Cleveland to Albany to visit family members and to pursue the things of the Spirit. However, when they arrived in Rochester, Parley was prompted to part from his wife for a season and stay in the area, for, he wrote, "I have a work to do in this region of country, and what it is, or how long it will take to perform it, I know not....

"[I] visited an old Baptist deacon by the name of Hamlin ... [and] he began to tell of a book ... in his possession, which had just been published. This book, he said, purported to have been originally written on plates ... of gold ... by a branch of the tribes of Israel; and to have been discovered and translated by a young man near Palmyra ... by the aid of visions, or the ministry of angels."[58]

The next morning, Deacon Hamlin obtained his copy for Parley, who wrote: "For the first time, my eyes beheld the 'BOOK OF MORMON' ... I opened it with eagerness, and read its title page. I then read the testimony of several witnesses in relation to the manner of its being found and translated.... I read all day; eating was a burden, I had no desire for food; sleep was a burden when the night came, for I preferred reading to sleep.

"As I read, the spirit of the Lord was upon me, and I knew and comprehended that the book was true, as plainly and manifestly as a man comprehends and knows that he exists. My joy was now full....

"I found that Jesus Christ, in his glorified resurrected body, had appeared to the remnant of Joseph on the continent of America, soon after his resurrection.... Surely, thought I, Jesus had *other sheep*, as he said to his Apostles of old; and here they were."[59]

After a few days of study and much interaction with Hyrum Smith, brother of the Prophet, Parley desired with all his heart to be baptized. The two walked twenty-five miles to Fayette. Parley wrote: "I found the little branch of the church in this place full of joy, faith, humility and charity. We rested that night, and on the next day [September 1, 1830] ... I was baptized by the hand of ... Oliver Cowdery ... in Seneca Lake.... The same evening ... I was ordained to the office of an Elder in the Church, which included authority to preach, baptize, administer the sacrament, administer the Holy Spirit, by the laying on of hands in the name of Jesus Christ and to take the lead of meetings of worship."[60]

Great joy filled the heart of twenty-three-year-old Parley as he learned, as thousands were about to learn, that God is "the same yesterday, and today, and forever." (Hebrews 13:8.)

The last light of the evening sun glows upon a fence on the Whitmer property in Fayette. Because of the success of missionary work in Ohio's Western Reserve, the headquarters of the Church were about to be moved there.

3 OUT OF POVERTY: A HOUSE FOR THE SON OF GOD

As Parley P. Pratt and others read the Book of Mormon, they developed a great interest in preaching to the Indians. These were the descendents of the Lamanites, that people spoken of in the book who were of the house of Israel, to whom special blessings were promised. "When, when is the time?" they wondered, and they took their question to Joseph. In October 1830, he asked the Lord, who answered by calling Parley, Ziba Peterson, Peter Whitmer Jr., and Oliver Cowdery on a mission to the farthermost reaches of the western United States, a mission to the Indians in Missouri.

The Lord said, "I myself will go with them and be in their midst; and I am their advocate with the Father, and nothing shall prevail against them." (D&C 32:2–3.)

On their journey west, Parley wanted to stop near Kirtland, Ohio, to see an old friend, powerful Reformed Baptist preacher Sidney Rigdon. Known for his polished skill as an orator, Sidney was much respected by the people in the area. Parley wrote, "We soon presented [Sidney] with a Book of Mormon, and related to him the history of the same."[1] The four missionaries requested that they be permitted to speak to his congregation.

Oliver Cowdery and Parley Pratt spoke with great power to the many assembled. "At the conclusion, elder Rigdon arose and stated to the congregation that the information they had that evening received, was of an extraordinary character, and certainly demanded their most serious consideration: and . . . 'to prove all things and hold fast that which is good' . . . and not turn against it . . . lest they should, possibly, resist the truth."[2]

Parley wrote: "We tarried in this region for some time, and devoted our time to the ministry, and visiting from house to house. At length Mr. Rigdon and many others became convinced that they had no authority to minister in the ordinances of God; and that they had not been legally baptized and ordained. They, therefore, came forward and were baptized by us, and received the gift of the Holy Ghost by the laying on of hands. . . .

"In two or three weeks from our arrival in the neighborhood with the news, we had baptized one hundred and twenty-seven souls, and this number soon increased to one thousand."[3]

Pages 84–85: Section of the original Erie Canal (circa 1825) one block from the main street in Palmyra, New York. This was the major transportation route for the Saints leaving the area to make the 250-mile journey to Kirtland, Ohio. Mules were used to pull the barges and boats along the canal, which ran a total of 363 miles through New York.

Left: Disciples of Christ meetinghouse in Mentor, Ohio, on the corner of Jackson and Mentor Avenues, where the great restorationist preacher, Sidney Rigdon, had a large congregration of believers in 1830. This church was built in the 1870s on the foundation of the original that stood here when the four missionaries arrived in Ohio. A large picture of Sidney Rigdon hangs in the foyer of this church, designating him as its first minister. Other preachers included Alexander Campbell, Walter Scott, and President James A. Garfield.

Above: The Chagrin River, which runs through Kirtland, Ohio. Many early baptisms were performed near this spot, including that of 38-year-old farmer John Murdock on November 5, 1830. "The Spirit of the Lord rested on me [as I read the Book of Mormon]," recorded John, "witnessing to me of the TRUTH of the work. . . . I told the servants of the Lord that I was ready to walk with them into the waters of baptism. . . . I came out of the water rejoicing and singing praises to God."[4]

Right: Isaac Morley farmhouse, Kirtland, Ohio. Isaac settled with his wife, Lucy, in Kirtland in 1812. The Morleys were early converts of the Church in Ohio. They invited the Prophet and Emma to live here when they arrived in Kirtland. The Smiths lived with the Morleys for about seven months. Fourteen revelations now included in the Doctrine and Covenants were received while Joseph lived here.

The gospel found fertile soil in Kirtland, Ohio. As one pioneer journal recorded: "The country for many miles around had been for centuries the hunting-ground of the Indians. . . . The forest-trees were of endless variety and of the tallest kinds . . . birds of varied plumage filled the air with their music, and the air itself was fragrant and invigorating."[5]

More invigorating still were the people, many of whom were searching the Bible, anxious to live as Christ had taught. A small community of these families had gathered together at longtime resident Isaac Morley's farm on the Kirtland Flats. They were experimenting with living a communal order, hoping that the Lord would restore authority to the earth from the heavens.

The four missionaries met with this small group of believers, all of whom embraced the message of the gospel. Lyman Wight recorded, "They brought the Book of Mormon to bear upon us, and the whole of the common stock family was baptized."[6]

The Newel K. Whitney Store at the intersection of Chillicothe and Chardon Roads in Kirtland, Ohio. Next door was the home of Orson Hyde. Originally called the Gilbert and Whitney Store, with Algernon Sidney Gilbert the senior partner, the store was built by Newel Whitney in 1823. It was a center of commerce in the area and was the local post office of the day. It would become the spiritual center of the Church in Kirtland for a few years.

Because of the rapid growth of the Church in Ohio and the increased opposition in New York, Joseph Smith was directed by the Lord to move the fledgling church to Ohio, about 250 miles away: "And inasmuch as my people shall assemble themselves at the Ohio, I have kept in store a blessing such as is not known among the children of men, and it shall be poured forth upon their heads. And from thence men shall go forth into all nations." (D&C 39:15.)

Preparations were made in New York for the removal of the Saints in three large groups, one from Colesville, one from Fayette, and the last from Manchester. These Saints left all of their familiar surroundings to follow this living Prophet. "And I consecrate unto them this land [Ohio] for a little season, until I, the Lord, shall provide for them otherwise . . . And the hour and the day is not given unto them, wherefore let them act upon this land as for years, and this shall turn unto them for their good." (D&C 51:16–17.)

Restored interior of the Newel K. Whitney Store. Included in the restoration are period items that would have been sold in the store. Post-office boxes are on the left. A stove helped to heat lower and upper rooms. In this room the Prophet and Brother Whitney met for the first time.

On a wintry day, the first part of February 1831, Joseph and six-months-pregnant Emma arrived in Kirtland in front of the Gilbert and Whitney Store. The junior partner of the establishment, Newel Kimball Whitney, and his wife, Elizabeth Ann, had recently joined the Church. Joseph sprang from the sleigh and walked into the store. With hand outstretched to the man at the counter, he said, "Newel K. Whitney! Thou art the man!"[7] This meant, "I know you; you are Newel K. Whitney." The surprised thirty-seven-year-old merchant said, "You have the advantage of me. I could not call you by name as you have me." "I am Joseph the Prophet. You've prayed me here, now what do you want of me?"[8] The Prophet, while yet in New York, had seen in vision Newel and Elizabeth praying for him to come to Kirtland.

The Lord told Joseph, "If thou shalt ask, thou shalt receive revelation upon revelation." (D&C 42:61.) With many questions about the kingdom, Joseph received eleven revelations within three months of his arrival in Ohio.

Absorbed in the Lord's work, Joseph and Emma were at the mercy of others for a place to live, staying with the Whitneys and then with the Morleys. At the end of April, Emma gave birth to twins, Thaddeus and Louisa, and, as God's purposes are not always known, these little ones lived only three hours.

On that same day, John Murdock's wife, Julia, also had twins but was taken in death during childbirth. John wondered how he could possibly care for these two infants and his five other children. Hearing of the Prophet and Emma's loss, he asked if the Smiths would take the care of his babies. Joseph and Emma adopted Julia and Joseph Murdock Smith, only nine days old.

During the spring of 1831, John and Elsa Johnson and others came to visit the Prophet out of curiosity. They lived about thirty miles south in Hiram, Ohio, and wanted to learn for themselves about this talk of the Book of Mormon and a restoration of the ancient truths of the gospel. While together, the group discussed whether some of the miraculous gifts of God were still on the earth. One in the party said, "Here is Mrs. Johnson with a lame arm; has God given any power to man on earth to cure her?"[9] The conversation changed to other subjects, and then, suddenly, the Prophet took Mrs. Johnson by the hand and said, "Woman, in the name of the Lord Jesus Christ I command thee to be whole."[10] The group was awestruck with the confidence and calm assurance with which he spoke. Mrs. Johnson at once lifted her rheumatic arm with ease after not having been able to move it freely for over two years. The next day she was able to do her washing without difficulty or pain.

The Johnsons invited the Prophet and his little family to come and live with them in Hiram. The offer was gratefully accepted, and on September 12, 1831, the move was made from the Morleys' to the Johnsons'.

Because the Book of Mormon had prophesied that many of the "plain and precious parts" of the Bible would be removed by evil men (1 Nephi 13:26), the Prophet had been poring over the Bible, translating verses that needed clarification. Joseph considered this translation and revision one of the branches of his calling, and he received many revelations concerning doctrines that had been lost.

The back steps of John Johnson's farmhouse in Hiram, Ohio, about 30 miles south of Kirtland. Note the original foundation and cut stone. The Johnsons opened their home to Joseph and Emma and their adopted twins, Julia and Joseph Murdock Smith.

The John Johnson farmhouse, home of the Prophet and his little family from September 12, 1831, to September 1832. Here eight special conferences of the Church were held. Here fifteen revelations were received that are now canonized in the Doctrine and Covenants. Here the Prophet and Sidney Rigdon would nearly be killed by a mob.

One cold day in February 1832, Joseph and Sidney were translating the scriptures when it became apparent to them that many important points touching the salvation of humanity had been taken from the Bible, or lost before it was compiled. This caused them to wonder about what the term *heaven* meant—for surely it referred to more kingdoms than one.

As they came to the twenty-ninth verse of the fifth chapter of John, the Spirit gave them this insight: "Speaking of the resurrection of the dead, concerning those who shall hear the voice of the Son of Man: and shall come forth; they who have done good, in the resurrection of the just; and they who have done evil, in the resurrection of the unjust." (D&C 76:15–17.) This caused Joseph and Sidney to marvel greatly, and a great vision opened to their view. Ten others were present; Philo Dibble recorded: "Joseph would, at intervals, say: 'What do I see?' as one might say while looking out the window and beholding what all in the room could not see. Then he would relate what he had seen or what he was looking at.

Then Sidney replied, 'I see the same.' Presently Sidney would say 'what do I see?' and would repeat what he had seen or was seeing, and Joseph would reply, 'I see the same.'

"This manner of conversation was repeated at short intervals to the end of the vision . . . which . . . was over an hour. . . . Joseph sat firmly and calmly all the time in the midst of a magnificent glory, but Sidney sat limp and pale, apparently as limber as a rag, observing which, Joseph remarked, smilingly, 'Sidney is not used to it as I am.'"[11]

They saw three kingdoms of glory where resurrected souls may dwell, and they learned how one can obtain the highest degree of glory. "[The vision went] so much beyond the narrow mindedness of men," Joseph wrote, "that, every honest man is constrained to exclaim; 'It came from God.'"[12] They saw Jesus Christ and heard a voice bearing record that He is the Only Begotten of the Father, "full of grace and truth." Joseph and Sidney recorded, "This is the testimony, last of all, which we give of him: That he lives!" (D&C 76:22.)

Restored revelation and translation room in the John Johnson farmhouse, southeast room upstairs. Wherever Joseph had a study or an office was the headquarters of the Church during this period. The great revelation and vision on the three degrees of glory was received while the Prophet and Sidney Rigdon were working on the translation of the Bible. Joseph called this vision, published as section 76 of the Doctrine and Covenants, a "transcript from the records of the eternal world."[13]

By November 1, 1831, Joseph had received a number of revelations, and a conference of the Church was held at the Johnson farm where a decision was made to publish the revelations in book form. A number of Church members declared their feelings about these revelations: "We . . . feel willing to bear testimony to all the world of mankind, to every creature upon the face of the earth, . . . that the Lord has borne record to our souls, through the Holy Ghost shed forth upon us, that these commandments were given by inspiration of God, and are profitable for all men, and are verily true."[14]

One common theme unites these revelations—a powerful witness and testimony of Jesus Christ—"his divinity, his majesty, his perfection, his love, and his redeeming power—[making] this book [now called The Doctrine and Covenants of The Church of Jesus Christ of Latter-day Saints] of great value to the human family and of more worth than the riches of the whole earth."[15] Joseph called this book "the foundation of the Church in these last days, and a benefit to the world, showing that the keys of the mysteries of the kingdom of our Savior are again entrusted to man."[16]

It was an awful responsibility to write in the name of the Lord,"[17] recorded Joseph in his history. And so it was; Joseph, like Moses or Elijah of old, spoke the words of the Lord to His people—to all who would hear His voice.

Among the revelations received was instruction to establish the Church in Jackson County, Missouri, and to begin to take the gospel throughout the United States. Joseph had been to Missouri during the summer of 1831. There, with Sidney Rigdon and others, he dedicated the land for the establishment of Zion and for the building of a temple to the Lord. Missionaries were now being called to go two by two as they had been in the ancient Church. Branches of the Church were being organized in many places.

"Surely the Lord God will do nothing, but he revealeth his secret unto his servants the prophets," said Amos in the Old Testament. (Amos 3:7.) The kingdom of God was being established again, "precept upon precept; line upon line." (Isaiah 28:10.)

Pages 96–97: Sunset at the Johnson farm in Hiram, Ohio. After dark, that terrible night of March 24, 1832, a mob of sixty men gathered to do whatever harm they could to the Prophet and to Sidney Rigdon, who lived just down the road.

Above: Bedroom of Joseph and Emma in the Johnson farmhouse, southwest room on the main floor. The mob burst through the door on the left and dragged Joseph from the trundle bed coming out from under the larger bed. Joseph had been caring for eleven-month-old Joseph. That night Joseph had suggested that Emma and baby Julia go into another room because little Joseph was the sicker of the twins. Joseph thought Emma could use some peaceful sleep.

In March of 1832, opposition rose to alarming levels. The Johnson farm and surrounding areas, originally a place of safety, became a gathering place for enemies of the Church. Late Saturday night, the 24th of March, a mob gathered to seek the life of the Prophet. Full of venom and hatred, they first tore Sidney Rigdon from his bed and dragged him by his heels with a horse, lacerating his head as it bumped across the rough, frozen ground.

At the Johnsons', Joseph rested on the trundle bed with little Joseph, who was sick with the measles. Emma and Julia were sleeping in another room when about a dozen men burst through the front door. Emma started screaming, "Murder," and before Joseph realized what was happening, the mob was dragging him out of the house. Powerful hands came from everywhere, holding his hair, shirt, pants, arms, and legs. As Joseph struggled, the men screamed that resistance would be met by death, and they seized his throat until he passed out.

As he came to, he saw Sidney unconscious on the ground and assumed that he was dead. Joseph began pleading for his own life, but the mob cried out, "Call on yer God for help, we'll show ye no mercy!"[18] The mob increased to fifty or sixty, coming at him like hungry wolves for a lamb, stripping his clothes from him and beating him severely. One man attacked him like a mad cat, scratching every part of his body and muttering, *"That's the way the Holy Ghost falls on folks."*[19] After covering Joseph's body with hot tar, they tried to shove the tar paddle into his mouth, nearly choking him. They also forced a vial of poison into his mouth, but Joseph crushed it, breaking one of his front teeth in the process. Covering him with feathers stolen from the Rigdon home, they left him for dead.

"I attempted to rise," wrote Joseph, "but fell again; I pulled the tar away from my lips, so that I could breathe more freely, and after a while I began to recover, and raised myself up, whereupon I saw two lights."[20] Joseph crept back, wounded and aching, to the Johnson home some three hundred yards away. As he came to the door in the dark, Emma saw his tar-covered body. Thinking he was covered with blood and that he had been crushed to pieces, she fainted. Joseph's friends spent the night scraping the tar from his tortured body so that by morning he was ready to be clothed. That morning being the Sabbath, and with flesh "all scarified and defaced,"[21] undaunted, he arose and preached a sermon on brotherly love and charity to a congregation that included several members of the mob. That afternoon he baptized three persons.

Five days later, eleven-month-old baby Joseph died of a cold contracted when the door flew open and the outside air chilled him the night of the mobbing. In three more days, though bereaved of his son and still recovering from the beating, Joseph, whose recuperative powers were phenomenal, left for Missouri to strengthen the Saints there.

Joseph said, "The envy and wrath of man have been my common lot all the days of my life." (D&C 127:2.) But "those who cannot endure persecution, and stand in the day of affliction, cannot stand in the day when the Son of God shall burst the veil, and appear in all the glory of His Father."[22]

The traditional site where Joseph was dragged by the mob and beaten severely, stripped, scratched, and tarred and feathered. Some in the mob were apostates turned against the Prophet. They took him approximately 60 rods (330 yards) from the house to do their evil deed. A local newspaper report called this action "a base transaction, an unlawful act, a work of darkness, a diabolical trick."[23]

Newel and Elizabeth Whitney had been working in Kirtland to remodel their store to provide a place for the Prophet and Emma and Julia to live so that they might be closer to the main body of the Saints. They prepared a kitchen, a study, a bedroom, and a room for meetings. Here, at last, Joseph and Emma could have a home, and they were deeply grateful.

Twenty-seven-year-old Joseph continued the translation of the Bible until it was finished in July 1833. During this time, the Church was growing rapidly both here and in Missouri. Joseph was sought after often to answer questions that would arise concerning order, doctrine, and procedures in the Church.

On many occasions, others were present as Joseph inquired of the Lord on these matters and received revelation. Parley Pratt recorded:

"Each sentence was uttered slowly and very distinctly, and with a pause between each, sufficiently long for it to be recorded, by an ordinary writer, in long hand. This was the manner in which all his written revelations were dictated and written. There was never any hesitation, reviewing, or reading back, in order to keep the run of the subject; neither did any of these communications undergo revisions, interlinings, or corrections. As he dictated them so they stood, so far as I have witnessed; and I was present to witness the dictation of several communications of several pages each."[24]

Joseph lived by faith and by every word that proceeded forth from the mouth of God. He had been learning lesson after lesson. As he wrote: "No month ever found me more busily engaged . . . but as my life consisted of activity and unyielding exertions, I made this my rule: *When the Lord commands, do it.*"[25]

Here indeed was a prophet of God, a mouthpiece for the Lord on the earth to speak the mind and will of God to the people. Joseph sometimes felt alone and misunderstood, but he was full of compassion for his fellowman. He declared, "I don't blame any one for not believing my history."[26]

By commandment, Joseph organized the School of the Prophets in 1833, meeting in the Whitney Store. The Lord gave specific instructions about how the students should conduct themselves. As they entered the school they were to greet each other, saying, "I salute you in the name of the Lord Jesus Christ, in token or remembrance of the everlasting covenant . . . in a determination that is fixed, immovable, and unchangeable, to be your friend and brother through the grace of God in the bonds of love." (D&C 88:133.)

The school was unlike any other. There the Lord could prepare His friends to warn the people, and they would be ready, "instructed more perfectly in theory, in principle, in doctrine, in the law of the gospel, in all things that pertain unto the kingdom of God . . . things which have been, things which are, things which must shortly come to pass; things which are at home, things which are abroad; the wars and the perplexities of the nations . . . and a knowledge also of countries and of kingdoms." (D&C 88:78–79.)

Pages 100–101: East light filters through windows in the restored revelation room of the Newel K. Whitney Store in Kirtland. Seventeen revelations were received here, now canonized. The table in the room belonged to Joseph Smith.

Left: Porch of the Newel K. Whitney Store in Kirtland, Ohio. When the Saints arrived in Northern Ohio, Kirtland was one of its largest townships with an estimated population of 3,230, about the same as nearby Cleveland.

Above: Upper room at the northeast corner of the Newel K. Whitney Store, where the School of the Prophets was first held. Students first focused on spiritual instruction but later studied Hebrew, history, government, grammar, and geography. Joseph promised the students of the school that the pure in heart would behold a heavenly vision, and indeed, many saw Jesus and even God the Father.

Above: Emma Smith's kitchen in the Newel K. Whitney Store, northeast corner on the main floor. Joseph and his wife always attracted visitors because of his calling as a Prophet, so Emma spent a good portion of her time entertaining and feeding guests. The smoke and tobacco of the School of the Prophets above the kitchen was annoying to Emma, so she talked to Joseph about it.

Right: Southeast room on the main floor of the Newel K. Whitney Store. Most floorboards in the store are originals dating to the 1820s. One can go beneath the store and see the original foundation rocks and log support beams. Lamps often had individualized patterns so that at night, when someone carried a lamp, the person could be recognized by the lamp's pattern.

When the students in the School of the Prophets assembled in the room above Emma's kitchen for instruction, "the first they did was to light their pipes, and, while smoking, talk about the great things of the kingdom, and spit all over the room, and as soon as the pipe was out of their mouths a large chew of tobacco would then be taken. Often when the Prophet entered the room . . . he would find himself in a cloud of tobacco smoke,"[27] recorded one of the students, Brigham Young. Emma complained to Joseph of "having to clean so filthy a floor."[28] She said, "It would be a good thing if a revelation could be had declaring the use of tobacco a sin."[29]

On the 27th of February, 1833, Joseph went into his study to pray about this situation. The Lord was ever generous to the Prophet and to His children who desired to know more concerning His will. What did the Lord want for his servants concerning the use of tobacco? The Lord revealed to Joseph a marvelous health law, given scores of years before science would demonstrate its wisdom. Zebedee Coltrin reported, "The Prophet Joseph . . . came in with that revelation in his hand. Out of the twenty two members that were there assembled, all used tobacco more or less, except two, Joseph read the revelation and when they heard it they all laid aside their pipes and use of tobacco."[30]

This "Word of Wisdom," given of the Lord, was "adapted to the capacity of the weak and the weakest of all saints, who are or can be called saints." (D&C 89:3.) It called for abstinence from tobacco, alcohol, tea, and coffee, and for the moderate use of meat, with encouragement in the use of herbs, fruits, and grains.

It was given as a commandment with promise of great blessings: "All saints who remember to keep and do these sayings, walking in obedience to the commandments, shall receive health in their navel and marrow to their bones; and shall find wisdom and great treasures of knowledge, even hidden treasures; and shall run and not be weary, and shall walk and not faint. And I, the Lord, give unto them a promise, that the destroying angel shall pass by them, as the children of Israel, and not slay them." (D&C 89:18–21.) This health law would serve in years to come to set the Saints apart from the rest of the world.

Hymns sung at the temple dedication emphasized the Saints' feelings: "In faith we'll rely on the arm of Jehovah/To guide through these last days of trouble and gloom."[45] Then the dedicatory prayer was offered by the Prophet Joseph: "We ask thee, Holy Father, in the name of Jesus Christ, the Son of thy bosom . . . to accept of this house. . . . For thou knowest that we have done this work through great tribulation; and out of our poverty we have given of our substance to build a house to thy name, that the Son of Man might have a place to manifest himself to his people." (D&C 109:4–5.)

The choir then rose to their feet and sang a hymn written for the occasion, thrilling every soul: "The Spirit of God like a fire is burning!/The latter-day glory begins to come forth;/The visions and blessings of old are returning,/The angels are coming to visit the earth./We'll sing and we'll shout with the armies of heaven—/Hosanna, hosanna to God and the Lamb!/Let glory to them in the highest be given,/Henceforth and forever: amen and amen!"[46]

Left: On April 3, 1836, Joseph Smith and Oliver Cowdery witnessed great visions on the other side of this window, including a visitation from the Son of God Himself. The Lord said, "Let the hearts of your brethren rejoice, and let the hearts of all my people rejoice, who have, with their might, built this house to my name. For behold, I have accepted this house, and my name shall be here." (D&C 110:6, 7.) His voice was as the sound of the rushing of great waters.

Above: The women worked hard to help build the temple. The Saints were so poor that most who worked on the building did not have sufficient clothes to wear. The women would sew and knit shirts for the workers, who gave one out of every seven days to work on the temple.

The spire of the Kirtland Temple stood 110 feet from the ground. Great efforts were made to protect the temple from mob violence and destruction. Much of the time, guards were placed around the building night and day; however, other powers were watching over the work. One brother, Roger Orton, recorded seeing "a mighty angel riding upon a horse of fire, with a flaming sword in his hand, followed by five others, encircling the house, and protecting the Saints . . . from the power of Satan and a host of evil spirits, which were striving to disturb the Saints."[47]

In the evening meeting, Brother George A. Smith arose and began to prophesy, "when a noise was heard like the sound of a rushing mighty wind, which filled the Temple, and all the congregation simultaneously arose, being moved upon by an invisible power; many began to speak in tongues and prophesy; others saw glorious visions; and I beheld," Joseph recorded, "the Temple was filled with angels, which fact I declared to the congregation. The people of the neighborhood came running together (hearing an unusual sound within, and seeing a bright light like a pillar of fire resting upon the Temple), and were astonished at what was taking place."[48] Eliza R. Snow wrote, "The ceremonies of that dedication may be rehearsed, but no mortal language can describe the heavenly manifestations of that memorable day. Angels appeared to some, while a sense of divine presence was realized by all present."[49]

The following Sabbath, April 3, 1836, a congregation of 1,000 gathered again. After much prayer and speaking, the veils were dropped around the pulpits, and Joseph and Oliver bowed themselves in solemn and silent prayer. They arose from their prayer, and a great vision opened to their view. Before them, on the breastwork of the pulpit, stood the risen Lord, and "under his feet was a paved work of pure gold, in color like amber." (D&C 110:2.)

Joseph heard Him say, "I am the first and the last. I am he who liveth, I am he who was slain; I am your advocate with the Father. . . . I have accepted this house, and my name shall be here; and I will manifest myself to my people in mercy in this house." (D&C 110:3–4, 7.)

Then the heavens were opened again to Joseph and Oliver, and Moses appeared before them and "committed unto [them] the keys of the gathering of Israel from the four parts of the earth, and the leading of the ten tribes from the land of the north." (D&C 110:11.)

After this Elias appeared and committed the dispensation of the gospel of Abraham to them. Then, Joseph wrote, "another great and glorious vision burst upon us; for Elijah the prophet . . . stood before us, and said: Behold, the time has fully come, which was spoken of by the mouth of Malachi—testifying that he [Elijah] should be sent, before the great and dreadful day of the Lord." (D&C 110:12–14.)

Presendia Huntington recalled an event that occurred during one of the meetings she had not attended. "A little girl came to my door and in wonder called me out, exclaiming, 'The meeting is on the top of the meeting house!' I went to the door, and there I saw on the temple angels clothed in white covering the roof from end to end."[50] With such rewards from the heavens for their sacrifices, many thought they had entered a time of peace where trouble was behind them. They were wrong, and their hopes were shortly crushed.

The Kirtland Safety Society had been formed as an independent banking system for the ever-growing Church. It issued its own bills and guaranteed their payment. Speculation was running high all over the country, and within a short time banks began to crash, suspending all payments to depositors. The Kirtland bank was not immune to this panic. Many who were not strong in faith seceded from the Church. Joseph had led in establishing the bank, and this caused much anger and hatred and even murderous thoughts to be directed at the Prophet. Several elders called a meeting in the temple in February 1837 for all who considered Joseph a fallen prophet. Faithful Brigham Young attended the meeting and testified that "Joseph was a Prophet, and I knew it, and that they might rail and slander him as much as they pleased; they could not destroy the appointment of the Prophet of God, they could only destroy their own authority, cut the thread that bound them to the Prophet and to God, and sink themselves to hell."[51]

The Prophet Joseph felt very alone. He was arrested many times, and charges were brought against him from every side. Where there had been great light and glorious manifestations from the heavens, there was now darkness and manifestations of evil. Joseph recorded, "It seemed as though all the powers of earth and hell were combining their influence in an especial manner to overthrow the Church at once, and make a final end."[52]

Joseph's life was now in grave danger, and, being warned by the Spirit, he decided to move immediately to Missouri. In the first half of 1838, more than sixteen hundred Saints left Kirtland and followed Joseph to Far West, Missouri. Ohio had been only a stopping place on this journey of faith.

Left: Joseph Smith's home for a short period in Kirtland, located just north of the temple. This was the headquarters of the Church, and as many as six revelations included in the Doctrine and Covenants were received here. This is where Zion's Camp was organized.

Above: The summer sun ready to set, with a silhouette of the Kirtland Temple. Apostasy was rampant in Kirtland; many were turning against the Prophet and the teachings of the Lord. While hundreds were falling away, the missionary work in England silently moved forward with thousands upon thousands embracing the truth and joining the Church.

4
MISSOURI: LOOKING FOR THE HIGH GROUND THROUGH THE REFINER'S FIRE

Pages 116–17: Looking southeast from altar site on Tower Hill at Adam-ondi-Ahman, Missouri, into the great valley below. The area is called Adam-ondi-Ahman because it is the place where Adam shall come to visit his people, or the Ancient of Days shall sit, as spoken of by Daniel the prophet. When Adam was 927 years old he gathered his righteous posterity here, likely numbering many millions, and blessed them. The Savior appeared and blessed Adam. Missouri is a place where not much physical evidence remains of the early days of the Church, but much can still be felt.

In 1830, the four missionaries called by revelation in New York made their way through the Kirtland, Ohio, area to the frontiers of Missouri. Not fifty miles out of Kirtland, being back in his home country, Parley P. Pratt was arrested on a frivolous charge and taken to trial late in the evening. He was ordered to prison, but in the morning, Parley requested to step out into the public square with the officer in charge.

"Mr. Peabody," said Parley, "are you good at a race?" "No," said he, "but my big bull dog is, and he has been trained to assist me in my office." At this Parley said, "Well, you compelled me to go a mile, I have gone with you two miles. You have given me an opportunity to preach, sing, and have also entertained me with lodging and breakfast. I must now go on my journey; if you are good at a race you can accompany me. I thank you for all your kindness—good day, sir."

Parley then started on his journey while the officer stood, amazed, not able to put one foot in front of the other. Parley wrote: "Seeing this, I halted, turned to him and again invited him to a race. He still stood amazed. I then renewed my exertions, and soon increased my speed to something like that of a deer. . . .

"He now came hallooing after me, and shouting to his dog to seize me. The dog, being one of the largest I ever saw, came close on my footsteps with all his fury; the officer behind still in pursuit, clapping his hands and hallooing, 'stu-boy, stu-boy—take him—watch—lay hold of him, I say—down with him,' and pointing his finger in the direction I was running. The dog was fast overtaking me, and in the act of leaping upon me, when, quick as lightning, the thought struck me, to assist the officer, in sending the dog with all fury to the forest a little distance before me. I pointed my finger in that direction, clapped my hands, and shouted in imitation of the officer. The dog hastened past me with redoubled speed towards the forest. . . . I soon lost sight of the officer and the dog. . . . I passed on six miles further, through mud and rain, and overtook the brethren, and preached that same evening to a crowded audience."[1]

"In the beginning of 1831 we renewed our journey; and, passing through St. Louis . . . we travelled on foot for three hundred

Old Jackson County Courthouse located in Independence, Missouri, circa 1827. The Lord designated the location of the great temple to be built in the New Jerusalem near here.

miles through vast prairies and . . . trackless wilds of snow—no beaten road; houses few and far between; and the bleak northwest wind always blowing in our faces with a keenness which would almost take the skin off the face. . . . We carried on our backs our changes of clothing, several books, and corn bread and raw pork. We often ate our frozen bread and pork by the way, when the bread would be so frozen that we could not bite or penetrate any part of it but the outside crust.

"After much fatigue and some suffering we all arrived in Independence, in the county of Jackson, on the extreme western frontiers of Missouri, and of the United States. This was about fifteen hundred miles from where we started . . . through a wilderness country, in the worst season of the year . . . during which we had preached the gospel to tens of thousands of Gentiles and two nations of Indians; baptizing, confirming and organizing many hundreds of people into churches of Latter-day Saints."[2]

Above: Noxious weeds grow in abundance in Missouri. On August 2, 1831, Sidney Rigdon dedicated the land for the gathering of the Saints. The next day, the spot for the temple was dedicated by the Prophet. The occasion was solemn and impressive, and the Spirit of the Lord was poured out in abundance.

Right: Honey-locust tree on the original 63.27 acres of land purchased by Edward Partridge in 1831 for the building of the temple in Independence, Missouri. These armored trees around the Saints' settlements could have slowed down the horses of the mobs riding in. In recent years over 10,000 of these trees have been logged from Adam-ondi-Ahman alone. The lieutenant governor of the state in 1831, Lilburn W. Boggs, was a large landowner in Jackson County. In the summer of 1833, he encouraged the residents to rise up against the Mormons.

Parley Pratt was chosen to return to Kirtland to report on their labors in Missouri. Word had been received in Missouri that Joseph and his family had moved to Ohio now, and most of the Saints in New York were moving as well. Parley made the long trek and was received in Kirtland by hundreds of welcoming Saints. He gave his report of their mission to the west, and within a short time the Lord revealed through Joseph that the next conference of the Church was to be held in Missouri "upon the land which I will consecrate unto my people." (D&C 52:2.)

In June 1831, the Lord began to give instructions to the Saints about Missouri in a vast, grand plan. Sidney Gilbert was called to be a land agent in western Missouri by setting up a store to sell goods and then use those funds to purchase lands "for the good of the saints." (D&C 57:8.) Edward Partridge was called as the first bishop in the Church to divide the properties among the Saints as they arrived. The Colesville Branch of the Church from New York desired to move as a group to Missouri to claim their inheritance.

The Prophet and others arrived in Independence near the end of July 1831, reunited with their friends amid tears of joy. A revelation was given about the building of Zion, that same Zion long awaited since ancient times: "Hearken, O ye elders of my church, saith the Lord your God, who have assembled yourselves together . . . in this land, which is the land of Missouri, which is the land which I have appointed and consecrated for the gathering of the saints. Wherefore, this is the land of promise, and the place for the city of Zion. . . . Behold, the place which is now called Independence is the center place; and a spot for the temple is lying westward, upon a lot which is not far from the courthouse." (D&C 57:1–3.)

On this occasion, the Prophet recorded, "Our reflections were many, coming as we had from a highly cultivated state of society in the east, and standing now upon the . . . western limits of the United States . . . how natural it was to observe the degradation, leanness of intellect, ferocity, and jealousy of a people that were nearly a century behind the times, and to feel for those who roamed about without the benefit of civilization, refinement, or religion."[3]

"The soil is rich and fertile," wrote Sidney Rigdon of Missouri. "As far as the eye can reach the beautiful rolling prairies lie spread out like a sea of meadows. . . . Buffalo, elk, deer, bear, wolves, beaver and many smaller animals here roam at pleasure. Turkey, geese, swans, ducks, yea a variety of the feathered tribe, are among the rich abundance that grace the delightful regions of this goodly land—the heritage of the children of God."[4]

On the 2nd of August, the Prophet assisted the Colesville Branch, numbering about sixty souls, in laying the first log for a house, as a foundation of Zion. Here would be the center "stake" of the tent of Israel, the place where the Lord would come to visit the earth once more.

Polly Knight, wife of Joseph Knight, had been sick on their fifteen-hundred-mile trek to Missouri, longing for only one thing: to set foot on the land of Zion and be buried there. Four days after the dedication of the temple lot, she died, having fulfilled her deepest desire.

Left: Long afternoon shadows of a modern fence on the original temple property in Independence, Missouri. The Saints tried to purchase as much land as possible in the area of Independence. The Lord told them, "Those that live shall inherit the earth, and those that die shall rest from all their labors." (D&C 59:2.)

Above: Broken wagon wheel on the temple land in Independence. When hostilities in Jackson County began, Bishop Edward Partridge and Charles Allen were dragged from their homes to the public square, where the mob demanded that Allen renounce the Book of Mormon and that Partridge leave the county. Both refused, and the mob violently tarred and feathered them. Bishop Partridge said calmly that he was willing to suffer for the sake of Christ as the Saints in former ages had done. The bishop bore the mobbing with such meekness that the crowd seemed awe-struck and allowed him to leave in silence.

The light of the setting sun illuminates this snow-covered patch of dried weeds, which now grow over the temple land in Independence where the great city of the New Jerusalem will be built. At the highest point of the original temple property, during the winter, one can see for 20 to 30 miles in every direction, this being one of the highest plots of ground in Western Missouri. Seven revelations of the Doctrine and Covenants were received near this spot.

By the summer of 1833, immigration of the Saints into Jackson County had increased to nearly a thousand people, with more arriving every week. It was a clash of cultures as these eastern folk, full of industry and desire to cultivate and subdue the wilderness, settled among the rough, backwoods frontier people of Missouri. The Saints "had all purchased lands and paid for them, and most of them were improving in buildings . . . and the wilderness became a fruitful field," recorded Parley Pratt.

"They lived in peace and quiet; no lawsuits with each other or with the world; few or no debts were contracted; few promises broken; there were no thieves, robbers, or murderers; few or no idlers; all seemed to worship God with a ready heart. On Sundays the people assembled to preach, pray, sing, and receive the ordinances of God. Other days all seemed busy in the various pursuits of industry. In short, there has seldom, if ever, been a happier people upon the earth than the Church of the Saints now were."[5]

Under some tall trees in a secluded place, a school of elders with some sixty enrolled met once a week to pray, preach, prophesy, and exercise the gifts of the Spirit. Many who gathered to this school came six to ten miles, often in bare feet, to be strengthened and to edify one another.

Still there was a warning in the air, an uneasy current. Through the Prophet Joseph, residing in Kirtland, the Lord said, "Ye cannot behold with your natural eyes, for the present time, the design of your God concerning those things which shall come hereafter, and the glory which shall follow after much tribulation. For after much tribulation come the blessings." (D&C 58:3–4.) Could tribulation be coming to these fruitful fields?

A whirlwind was stirring in the hearts of old-time Jackson County residents, who began to be increasingly suspicious as the new settlers swelled in number. Many feared that they would be outnumbered by the religiously motivated settlers from the East. It was easy to predict that with a few hundred more Saints, they could change the political scene and wrest control of the county.

Entrepreneurial Saints took over some of the Santa Fe Trail trade business from local residents with considerable success. They established a printing business, and *The Evening and Morning Star*, the first periodical in the area, was published. Because this was an exclusive newspaper, catering to the needs of the Saints, local and national issues were represented from that point of view. Some of the Saints, too, boasted that a great many more members of the Church would be arriving soon to claim their inheritance in Zion. This caused great alarm among the locals.

The Missouri frontiersmen hated the Indians, while the Saints claimed the Indians to be one of the tribes of Israel and a chosen people. The Missourians were slave owners while the Saints were against slavery. This last issue became especially hot when an article was published in the *Star* cautioning missionaries about proselyting among former slaves, known as "free people of color." The Missourians misinterpreted the article as encouragement for slaves to join the Saints in western Missouri, and they felt pushed about as far as they could go.

Pages 126–27: Low-lying Jackson County field with stubble of corn in winter. The Mormons made their way across such fields as they were driven from the county. "Mormon" was a nickname given by the persecutors of the Saints to identify anyone associated with Joseph Smith and the Book of Mormon; similarly were the Saints in the time of the Savior called "Christian" by their persecutors for following Jesus Christ.

During the summer of 1833, hundreds of Missourians circulated a "secret constitution" denouncing the Mormons. In July, about five hundred Missourians gathered at the Independence courthouse to draft a document outlining their demands and to issue a bitter ultimatum that no Latter-day Saints would be allowed to move to or settle in Jackson County and that those who were already there must pledge to leave in a reasonable time. The document also called for the immediate cessation of the Church newspaper. The leaders of the Church, upon receiving the demands, asked for three months to consider the proposition and consult with Church leaders in Ohio. This request was denied, and they pleaded for ten days. This was also denied, and the Saints were given fifteen minutes to look over and agree to the resolution.

This meeting quickly erupted from discussions into an angry mob as the Missourians, smoldering with resentment, decided to immediately implement a resolution to destroy the printing press. They went en masse to the printing office and the residence of the publisher, W. W. Phelps. They threw furniture into the street and garden, destroyed and hauled away the press, scattered type everywhere, and threw the printing job in process out of the building into piles to be burned. This was the sacred Book of Commandments, a publication of the revelations given to Joseph Smith to this point.

Two sisters, Mary Elizabeth and Caroline Rollins, ages fourteen and twelve, watched from their hiding place as the mob threw all the unbound copies of the book out of the printing office and began to level the two-story building. Wanting to save as many of the sheets as possible, they scooped what they could carry into their arms and ran behind the building. The mob spotted them and shouted for them to stop as they frantically ran and hid in a nearby cornfield. For a long time they heard the men searching for them, but they lay quietly on the ground until the mob left. These few copies preserved from this first printing have become priceless symbols of courage.

Mob violence continued to erupt in Jackson County until it reached a fever pitch. Mobs boldly attacked several settlements, "bursting into houses without fear . . . frightening women and children, and threatening to kill them if they did not flee immediately."⁶

In a cornfield battle, many were injured, including Philo Dibble, who was shot through his waistband. The ball remained inside him; "he bled much inwardly, and, in a day or two his bowels were so filled with blood and so inflamed that he was about to die. . . . Elder Newel Knight administered to him, by the laying on of hands, in the name of Jesus; his hands had scarcely touched his head when he felt an operation penetrating his whole system as if it had been a purifying fire. He immediately discharged several quarts of blood and corruption, among which was the ball. . . . He was instantly healed, and went to work chopping wood."⁷

Two Missourians were killed during the skirmish, which enraged the mob to unprecedented levels. The Saints began to run for their lives. Within the next three days, all the Mormons were driven from the county; houses were burned, fields trampled, and personal belongings destroyed. More than two hundred homes were burned to the ground; orchards were destroyed, fields of crops decimated, belongings stolen or pillaged. The shores of the Missouri River became swollen with refugees on both sides.

The mobs rejoiced as they saw the Mormons driven north to Clay County out of their midst. Lyman Wight recorded, "I saw one hundred and ninety women and children driven thirty miles across the prairie . . . the ground thinly crusted with sleet; and I could easily follow on their trail by the *blood that flowed from their lacerated feet* on the stubble of the burnt prairie!"⁸ Emily Austin wrote: "We lived in tents until winter set in, and did our cooking out in the wind and storms. Log heaps were our parlor stoves, and the cold, wet ground our velvet carpets, and the crying of little children our piano forte."⁹ As the Saints lay on the banks of the mighty Missouri River, they mourned: "By the rivers of Babylon, there we sat down, yea, we wept, when we remembered Zion." (Psalm 137:1.)

128

Twelve hundred homeless Saints were scattered through the counties of Missouri, their dream of a Zion at the center place vanished like smoke on the wind. Elizabeth Haven, who endured many persecutions, recorded in a letter to a friend: "God moves in a mysterious way, his wonders to perform. Many have been sifted out of the Church, while others have been rooted . . . in love and are the salt of the earth. . . . We are to be tried (everyone who inhabits the celestial kingdom) like gold seven times purified."[10] "That the trial of your faith," the apostle Peter admonished, "being much more precious than of gold that perisheth, though it be tried with fire, might be found unto praise and honour and glory at the appearing of Jesus Christ." (1 Peter 1:7.)

Now what were they to do? The Lord had told Joseph Smith: "Zion shall be redeemed, although she is chastened for a little season. . . . Let your hearts be comforted; for all things shall work together for good to them that walk uprightly." (D&C 100:13, 15.)

During the 1834 winter, a conference of the Saints was held in the shanty of Parley Pratt, where it was decided to send Parley and Lyman Wight to Kirtland to seek counsel and aid. Parley recorded: "I was at this time entirely destitute of proper clothing for the journey; and I had neither horse, saddle, bridle, money nor provisions to take with me; or to leave with my wife, who lay sick and helpless most of the time. . . . I knew not what to do. Nearly all had been robbed and plundered, and all were poor . . . it seemed to be all but an impossibility. . . . At length . . . the Spirit whispered to me, 'is there anything too hard for the Lord?'"[11]

Parley went from family to family and individual to individual, each in succession being touched by the Spirit to help him. "'There comes brother Parley; he's in want of a horse for his journey—I must let him have old Dick'; this being the name of the best horse he had. 'Yes,' said I, 'brother, you have guessed right; but what will I do for a saddle?' 'Well,' says the other, 'I believe I'll have to let you have mine.' I blessed them and went on my way rejoicing."[12] All of Parley and Lyman's needs were seen to, and they left to bring word of the persecutions, mobbings, and property losses to the leadership of the Church at Kirtland.

Pages 128–29: Clouds at sunset over the Missouri River bordering Jackson and Clay counties. "When night again closed upon us . . . hundreds of people were seen in every direction, some in tents and some in the open air around their fires, while the rain descended in torrents. Husbands were inquiring for their wives, wives for their husbands; parents for children, and children for parents."[13]

Left: This field at Far West, Missouri, used to be covered with a thriving community of homes, shops, hotels, businesses, and trades. The temple was to be built on the brow of the hill where the trees can be seen.

Above: Old road in northern Missouri like that traveled by Parley Pratt and Lyman Wight as they returned to Kirtland to give reports to the leadership of the Church of the conditions and trials of the Saints in Missouri.

Above: About four miles from Greencastle, Indiana. Period cabin, circa 1825, along the Zion's Camp trail. "Threatened by their enemies that they should not pass through Indianapolis, when near the place many got into the wagons, and, separating some little distance, passed through the city, while others walked down different streets, leaving the inhabitants wondering 'when that big company would come along.'"[14]

Right: "Saturday, May 24. [1834]—We crossed the Wabash River at Clinton [Indiana] in ferry boats, in quick time, and pushed on to the state line, where we arrived late in the evening, and encamped in an oak opening in Edgar County, Illinois."[15] Crossing a river was always a major undertaking. Zion's Camp was a time for the Prophet to teach the 204 men, 11 women, and 7 children in the camp about the dealings of God with His children.

When the Ohio Saints heard of the plight of their suffering friends in Missouri, they wanted to help. A commandment was given that at least one hundred "of the strength of my house" be gathered to go as an army of the Lord to help them recover their lands and homes in Missouri. (D&C 103:22.) Many gathered to heed the call, but little money was available for them to make the journey. Wilford Woodruff, a convert of four months, recorded: "He [Joseph] said . . . 'Brethren, don't be discouraged about our not having means. The Lord will provide, and He will put it into the heart of somebody to send me some money.' The very next day he received a letter from Sister Vose, containing one hundred and fifty dollars. When he opened the letter and took out the money, he held it up and exclaimed: 'See here, did I not tell you the Lord would send me some money to help us on our journey? Here it is.' I felt satisfied that Joseph was a Prophet of God in very deed."[16]

Joseph spoke to the group before leaving: "I want to say to you before the Lord, that you know no more concerning the destinies of this Church and kingdom than a babe upon its mother's lap. You don't comprehend it. It is only a little handful . . . you see here tonight, but this Church will fill North and South America—it will fill the world. It will fill the Rocky Mountains. There will be tens of thousands of Latter-day Saints who will be gathered in the Rocky Mountains."[17]

The little group of a hundred departed on their thousand-mile march to western Missouri, calling themselves "Zion's Camp." They armed themselves with weapons, many supplies, and great faith. Within a few weeks another group, recruited by Hyrum Smith, joined the march, swelling the ranks to over two hundred. Such a scene was not common on the frontiers of America, and curiosity and threats plagued the group all along the way. Spies made every effort to discover their identity, their destination, their objective, and their leaders. "My boy, where are you from?" "From the East." "Where are you going?" "To the West." "What for?" "To see where we can get land cheapest and best." "Who leads the camp?" "Sometimes one, sometimes another."[18] For security reasons, Joseph was given twenty men to be his personal bodyguards.

"It was a great school for us to be led by a Prophet of God a thousand miles through cities, towns, villages, and through the wilderness," wrote Wilford Woodruff. "When persons stood up to count us, they could not tell how many we numbered. Some said five hundred, others, a thousand."[19] This journey was a time of learning for all the men and women involved in the camp.

On one occasion, three prairie rattlesnakes were found in the spot where Joseph had pitched his tent. Some of the brethren were about to kill them, but Joseph said: "Let them alone—don't hurt them! How will the serpent ever lose his venom, while the servants of God possess the same disposition, and continue to make war upon it?" The brethren took the snakes carefully on sticks and carried them across the creek to safety. Joseph felt that "men must become harmless, before the brute creation; and when men lose their vicious dispositions . . . the lion and the lamb can dwell together, and the sucking child can play with the serpent in safety."[20]

"Notwithstanding our enemies were continually breathing threats of violence," wrote Joseph, "we did not fear, neither did we hesitate to [take] our journey, for God was with us, and His angels went before us, and the faith of our little band was unwavering."[21]

Ready to go to battle against those who had taken away the homes of the Saints in Missouri, the army arrived in the western part of the state some seven weeks after leaving Kirtland. Nearby, mobs from surrounding counties had gathered in great numbers to seek the destruction of the Zion's Camp band. Five marauders rode wildly through the camp to warn them of their impending doom.

When the five men entered the camp, not a cloud was to be seen in the whole heavens, but soon a small cloud like a black spot appeared in the northwest and began to unroll itself like a scroll. In a few minutes, the whole heavens were covered with a pall as black as ink. The storm soon broke with wind, rain, thunder, lightning, and hail. Many Saints fled to a nearby Baptist meetinghouse. Wilford Woodruff remembered: "As the Prophet Joseph came in shaking the water from his hat and clothing he said, 'Boys, there is some meaning to this. God is in this storm.' We sang praises to God, and lay all night on benches under cover while our enemies were in the pelting storm."[22]

Left: Old period barn along the Zion's Camp march near Mansfield, Indiana. The camp would often make 20 to 30 miles in a day and try to find a small woods or clearing where they could camp in safety. Trees could not grow in the long stretches of prairie grass.

Pages 136–37: Fishing River, Missouri, site of Zion's Camp. At this spot on June 22, 1834, a revelation was received. The Lord said: "It is expedient in me that mine elders should wait for a little season, for the redemption of Zion. For behold, I do not require at their hands to fight the battles of Zion; for . . . I will fight your battles." (D&C 105:13, 14.) The Lord also said through the Prophet, "There has been a day of calling, but the time has come for a day of choosing; and let those be chosen that are worthy." (D&C 105:35.)

Very little hail fell in our camp . . . the lightning flashed incessantly. . . . The earth trembled and quaked, the rain fell in torrents, and, united, it seemed as if the mandate of vengeance had gone forth from the God of battles."[23] The water in nearby Big Fishing River, which had been only ankle deep the night before, had risen to forty feet deep, drowned some of the mob, and sent the others running for shelter and galloping off to their homes. They declared that if that was the way God fought for the Mormons, they might as well go about their business.[24]

While their enemies attacked them from without, a deadly enemy attacked the army from within. Cholera broke out, ravaging about sixty-eight of the men and women, fourteen of whom died. The brethren rolled the corpses in blankets and buried them on the bank of Brush Creek. Heber C. Kimball remembered, "We felt to sit and weep over our brethren, and so great was our sorrow that we could have washed them with our tears, to realize that they had traveled one thousand miles through so much fatigue to lay down their lives for our brethren."[25]

A few days later, Zion's Camp was disbanded, unable to help their displaced brothers and sisters. Back in Kirtland, in 1835, Joseph called a meeting of all those who had been a part of Zion's Camp, saying, "God had not designed all this for nothing, but He had it in remembrance yet; and it was the will of God that those who went to Zion, with a determination to lay down their lives, if necessary, should be ordained to the ministry . . . to prune the vineyard for the last time, for the coming of the Lord, which was nigh."

He said, "Some of you are angry with me, because you did not fight in Missouri; but let me tell you, God did not want you to fight. He could not organize His kingdom with twelve men to open the Gospel door to the nations of the earth, and with seventy men under their direction to follow in their tracks, unless He took them from a body of men who had offered their lives, and who had made as great a sacrifice as did Abraham. Now the Lord has got His Twelve and His Seventy."[26]

Though the citizens of Clay County were at first hospitable and kind to the Saints, it was not long before they began to feel that these spiritual refugees needed to find homes and work elsewhere. Citizens met in Clay, Ray, Clinton, and other counties, plotting to deprive the Saints of their rights and drive them from the counties.

Finally, Alexander Doniphan, a state legislator and loyal friend to the Saints, introduced a bill for the creation of two small counties in the northern part of large Ray County, one to be a home for the Mormons. A buffer some six miles between the counties was created where no one would be allowed to settle. After being homeless for nearly three years, the Saints flowed into Caldwell and also Daviess counties by the thousands, seeking refuge and strength in the security of their numbers.

W. W. Phelps and John Whitmer located a site for a city in the northern prairie of Ray County, naming it Far West. Using money that had been collected from branches of the Church for "bleeding Zion," they purchased land for a town site.

The Lord told Joseph in Far West "that the gathering together upon the land of Zion, and upon her stakes, may be for a defense, and for a refuge from the storm, and from wrath. . . . Let the city, Far West, be a holy and consecrated land unto me. . . . It is my will that the city . . . should be built up speedily by the gathering of my saints." (D&C 115:6–7, 17.)

The plat for the city of Far West was a pattern for Zion, given to the Saints by the Prophet Joseph Smith. It was laid out with one square mile of land, with streets aligned to the compass, running north and south, east and west, and forming 3.6-acre blocks. A temple would be built in the center of the city, and all the locations in the town would be measured by their distance away from this central block.

What had once been a lonely prairie, where the winds blew through the grasses, became almost overnight a bustling community. As persecutions increased in Ohio, Kirtland Saints streamed in. Homeless Missouri Saints came looking for stability, and in March 1838, Joseph and six-months-pregnant Emma joined the members thronging to Far West.

Dances of the stars at Adam-ondi-Ahman. The North Star—Polaris, in the center—is a symbol of the constancy of Christ. Joseph's interest in and love of the stars were only heightened by his discovery of some ancient papyrus from Egypt containing a record written by Abraham of some of the lessons of astronomy from the Lord Himself. This papyrus was translated and later became the Book of Abraham now canonized in the Pearl of Great Price. Joseph had learned in Kirtland that Christ's light was in the sun, the moon, and the stars, and that this light "proceedeth forth from the presence of God to fill the immensity of space—the light which is in all things, which giveth life to all things, which is the law by which all things are governed, even the power of God." (See D&C 88:7, 12, 13.)

Southwest cornerstone of the Far West Temple. The Lord had commanded the saints to build a temple here, but the mobs and persecutions became so intense that the task became impossible to complete at that time. "During the time I was in the hands of my enemies," Joseph recorded, ". . . I felt perfectly calm, and resigned to the will of my Heavenly Father."[27] Seven canonized revelations were received in Far West.

Joseph's presence was a solace and a sustaining power to the Saints. He animated them by the courage of his presence and taught them patience by his own tenacity and endurance," said George Q. Cannon. "He was not there as a warrior; he did not bear arms; and yet he was a tower of strength to his [people]."[28]

This was a time for the Saints, with unflinching spirit, to begin again, plowing fields and laying cornerstones, establishing other settlements at Haun's Mill and DeWitt.

Caldwell County in 1836 was a wilderness. By the spring of 1838 the population was more than 5,000 of which more than 4,900 were Latter-day Saints with the greater concentration at Far West which by this time had 150 houses, four dry goods stores, three family groceries, half-a-dozen blacksmith shops, a printing establishment and two hotels. A large and comfortable schoolhouse had been built in 1836 and served also as a church and courthouse.[29]

Having lost the temple in Kirtland, Joseph had uppermost in his mind the goal of building another temple. Upon the Lord's command, cornerstones were laid July 4, 1838, with great fanfare, and the walls of the temple began to climb. The ceremony was held under the waving American flag. "We then and there declared our constitutional rights as American citizens," Parley recorded, "and manifested our determination to resist, with our utmost endeavors from that time forth, all oppression, and to maintain our rights and our freedom, according to the holy principles of liberty, as guaranteed to every person by the Constitution and laws of our country."[30]

During the few untroubled days at Far West, important revelations were given to the young Church. The law of tithing was reintroduced from the ancient times, which was a giving of one-tenth of one's increase (income) annually to the Lord. The strict adherence to this sacred law would later free the debt-laden Church from all encumbrances of the world, but Joseph would not live to see that day.

The official name of the Church was revealed in Far West: "For thus shall my church be called in the last days, even The Church of Jesus Christ of Latter-day Saints." (D&C 115:4.) At the time of the ministry of the Savior upon the earth, too, his church was called after his name, with members referred to as "Saints." "And how be it my church save it be called in my name? For if a church be called in Moses' name then it be Moses' church; or if it be called in the name of a man then it be the church of a man; but if it be called in my name then it is my church, if it so be that they are built upon my gospel." (3 Nephi 27:8.)

While Joseph was laying out this city, apostasy began to rage within the ranks of the Church. Jealousies, pride, and insurrections overcame some of the most powerful leaders of the Church, including David Whitmer, Oliver Cowdery, W. W. Phelps, Luke Johnson, and others, some of whom had been charged with using Church funds to obtain personal profit. Joseph's heart broke to see many of these once-loyal friends turn against him and the Church, to see them excommunicated. Joseph's life now was nearly always in danger from without and within the Church.

Detail of the southeast cornerstone of the Far West Temple in the fall. The Saints wondered about not being able to build the temples at Far West, Adam-ondi-Ahman, and Independence. But the Lord explained, "When I give a commandment to any of the sons of men to do a work unto my name, and those sons of men go with all their might and with all they have to perform that work, and cease not their diligence, and their enemies come upon them and hinder them from performing that work, behold, it behooveth me to require that work no more at the hands of those sons of men, but to accept of their offerings." (D&C 124:49.)

Affidavits and letters that apostate William Phelps had written led to much suffering and hardship for the Saints in Far West. When he later came back repentant, desiring to have full fellowship again with the Saints, Joseph wrote to him with compassion and charity: "It is true, that we have suffered much in consequence of your behavior—the cup of gall, already full enough for mortals to drink, was indeed filled to overflowing when you turned against us. One with whom we had oft taken sweet counsel together, and enjoyed many refreshing seasons from the Lord—'had it been an enemy, we could have borne it. . . .'

"However, the cup has been drunk, the will of our Father has been done. . . . I shall be happy once again to give you the right hand of fellowship, and rejoice in the returning prodigal. . . .

"Come on, dear brother, since the war is past, For friends at first, are friends again at last."[31] William Phelps ever remembered the kindness and loving forgiveness of the Prophet and the Lord.

Left: Light touching some of the sacred ground at Adam-ondi-Ahman. Near this spot Lyman Wight had a home and ran a ferry across the Grand River. The Prophet Joseph came here in 1838 to determine if a community of Saints could be established, and his survey party laid out a city with a square, a temple site, businesses, and homes. More than 2,000 people flocked to this area. The community did not last long before they were driven out by the angry mobs.

Above: Two black walnut trees have grown together as one on this spot on Tower Hill at Adam-ondi-Ahman. Joseph named this place Tower Hill because of an old "Nephitish" altar or tower found near this spot when he and his party arrived. Joseph said the altar was on the site where Adam and Eve offered sacrifice to the Lord and where they were taught by holy messengers about heavenly truths.

As the Saints began to assemble in Far West, "the war clouds began again to lower with dark and threatening aspect," recorded Parley P. Pratt. "Those who had combined against the laws in the adjoining counties, had long watched our increasing power and prosperity with jealousy, and with greedy and avaricious eyes. It was a common boast that, as soon as we had completed our extensive improvements, and made a plentiful crop, they would drive us from the state, and once more enrich themselves with the spoils."[32]

One day the Prophet was at his parents' home writing letters. "While he was thus engaged," his mother recorded, "I beheld a large company of armed men advancing . . . eight of them came into the house. . . . 'We have come here to kill Joe Smith and all the "Mormons."' . . . 'I suppose,' said I, 'you intend to kill me, with the rest?' 'Yes, we do,' returned the officer. 'Very well,' I continued, 'I want you to act the gentleman about it, and do the job quick. Just shoot me down at once, then I shall be at rest; but I should not like to be murdered by inches.' 'There it is again,' said he. 'You tell a "Mormon" that you will kill him, and they will always tell you, "that is nothing—if you kill us, we shall be happy."'

"Joseph, just at that moment finished his letter, and, seeing that he was at liberty, I said, 'Gentlemen, suffer me to make you acquainted with Joseph Smith, the Prophet.' They stared at him as if he were a spectre. He smiled, and stepping towards them, gave each of them his hand, in a manner which convinced them that he was neither a guilty criminal nor yet a hypocrite." Joseph spoke to them at length about the things the Saints had suffered and then "he said, 'Mother, I believe I will go home now—Emma will be expecting me.' At this two of the men sprang to their feet, and declared that he should not go alone, as it would be unsafe—that they would go with him, in order to protect him." At the doorway, Lucy heard the conversation of the remaining guards about Joseph: "Did you not feel strangely when Smith took you by the hand? I never felt so in my life." "I could not move. I would not harm a hair of that man's head for the whole world." "This is the last time you will catch me coming to kill Joe Smith, or the 'Mormons' either."[33]

Pages 144–45: Forgotten cemetery site of nearly 300 early Saints about one mile west of Far West, likely where apostle David Patten was buried. No stones or markers are left here now, and the plot is used for growing alfalfa and corn. Few ironies in the history of the United States are as great as when 3,000 Missouri militia were ordered to lay siege to this city of American citizens and to murder its leaders. The temple site at Far West can be seen in the distance in the trees to the left of the white building.

Lyman Wight had been running the ferry across the Grand River about thirty-five miles north of Far West, and many Saints had gathered there to form a settlement. When the Prophet came to see if it would be a suitable spot for building another city, he looked over the vast valley and was overcome by the Spirit. This, he said, was the place where Adam and Eve lived after they were cast from the Garden of Eden. Spring Hill, near Lyman's home, "is named by the Lord Adam-ondi-Ahman, because . . . it is the place where Adam shall come [again] to visit his people." (D&C 116.) Within months, this new place of refuge swelled to more than 2,000 residents. Here in this sparsely settled area would be a cover from the storm they had always faced.

To the great chagrin of the Saints, however, their avowed enemy in Jackson County, Lilburn W. Boggs, was elected governor of the state. In "Diahman" (short for Adam-ondi-Ahman), the members of the Church wanted to be sure that they elected their own represen-

Above: Early morning steals across the valley of Adam-ondi-Ahman. In this place in the last days a meeting will be held where all the faithful Saints of all generations of the earth will gather and commune together. All the keys and stewardships of all who have held them will be given over to Adam, who is Michael, and he will in turn give them to the great Jehovah—Jesus Christ. This is one of the major events of the second coming of the Lord and will take place in this secluded, quiet valley in northwestern Missouri.

tative to serve in state government. Local resident William Peniston was a staunch foe of the Saints and desired to be elected against a far greater ratio of Mormons to non-Mormons.

The day of the election arrived, August 6, 1838, and Peniston addressed a crowd of voters in Gallatin (four miles south of Diahman), which at that time was a small row of "ten houses, three of which were saloons."[34] Hoping to excite the crowd against the Mormons, he shouted, "The Mormon leaders are a set of horse thieves, liars, counterfeiters, and you know they profess to heal the sick, and cast out devils, and you all know that is a lie."[35] With this kind of a speech, emotions ran high, and Dick Welding, a mob bully, punched one of the Saints to the ground. A fight broke out on all sides, with Mormon John Butler grabbing an oak stake from a woodpile and striking Missourians to the ground. Many people on both sides were seriously injured. Though few Mormons braved voting that day, Peniston still lost the election.

147

Crooked River, Missouri, where apostle David Patten and two others were killed in a clash with the organized mobs. The site of the battle was in the distance near the clearing in the trees to the right of the visible part of Crooked River. The last week of October 1838 was a time of great uprisings against the Saints, and the infamous "extermination order" was issued by Governor Boggs. Ironically, though it was not actively enforced, the order was not rescinded until 1976 by Governor Christopher "Kit" Bond.

After the election-day incident, relations between the Latter-day Saints and their anti-Mormon neighbors deteriorated rapidly. The Prophet tried to calm the hostility that had arisen in the area, visiting Adam Black, the newly elected judge for Daviess County, and pleading with him to sign an agreement of peace.

It was a worthless scrap of paper whose promise lasted less than twenty-four hours. Distorted stories spread like a prairie fire, further enflaming the mob spirit. "Smith has organized an army of five hundred men to exterminate the old settlers," they said.

Smoldering emotions turned to violence against the Saints. Hyrum Smith testified in an affidavit that several Mormons were whipped and that their bodies were lacerated with hickory withes, as well as being tied to trees and deprived of food.[36] Joseph noted families scattered from their homes and said, "My feelings were such as I cannot describe when I saw them flock into the village, almost entirely destitute of clothes."[37]

When the Saints appealed to Governor Boggs for relief, he said, "The quarrel was between the Mormons and the mob," and that they "might fight it out."[38]

Emboldened by the governor's apathy, a mass of anti-Mormon forces marched on Caldwell and Daviess counties to force the Mormons out. When word reached Far West of an attack upon the Mormons, the Caldwell County judge ordered Colonel Hinckle of Far West to send out a company to disperse the mob and rescue the prisoners.

As dawn approached on October 25, 1838, the militia from Far West engaged in battle at Crooked River, and three of the Mormons, including David W. Patten of the Council of the Twelve, were killed. The clash gave Boggs, a longtime enemy of the Saints, the excuse he had been waiting for. He claimed that the Saints had initiated hostilities, therefore, he wrote by executive order, "The Mormons must be treated as enemies and *must be exterminated* or driven from the state, if necessary for the public good."[39]

Parley P. Pratt complained of the order: "It said nothing of criminals; it made no allusion to punishing crime and protecting innocence; it was sufficient to be called a *'Mormon.'* A peaceable family just emigrating, or passing through the country; a missionary going or coming on his peaceable errand of mercy; an aged soldier of the American revolution on his death bed . . . a widow with her babes; the tender wife, or helpless orphan; all were included in this order of wholesale extermination or banishment."[40]

Extermination began, just three days after the governor's order, at Haun's Mill, a small settlement, where at 4:00 P.M. children were playing on either side of the creek and mothers were involved in domestic duties. Suddenly the sound of one hundred rifles crashed through the air as the mob shot mercilessly at everything in sight. Amanda Barnes Smith and her daughters saved their lives by running to the woods with bullets whistling by "like hailstones." But when she crept back to the mill, she saw her husband and ten-year-old son "lifeless upon the ground." Then she found another son shot in the head under the blacksmith's bellows where he had attempted to hide.[41] Nineteen people were massacred.

Millstone in Breckenridge, Missouri, taken from Jacob Haun's mill in a settlement of Saints consisting of about 200 souls. The Prophet had warned the families here that they should flee to Far West to the main body of the Saints for protection or their lives could be in danger. The Saints did not act upon that warning, and on Tuesday, October 30, 1838, the little settlement was attacked by a mob who fired between 1,600 and 1,700 balls at the homes, livestock, belongings, and people of the town. The settlement was decimated.

The storm of war had been building all around Far West. Mob activity had been so intense that Mercy Rachel Thompson wrote, "At times I feared to lay my Babe down lest they should slay me and leave it to suffer worse than immediate Death."[42]

By October 31, 1838, the anti-Mormon militia of up to three thousand gathering around the barricaded city outnumbered the Far West militia five to one. Commanding General Lucas sent a flag of truce to Colonel Hinckle, who secretly agreed to turn Joseph and other key leaders over for trial and punishment. He also agreed that Mormon property would be confiscated for damages and that the Saints would surrender their arms and leave the state.

In Far West, Hinckle told Joseph, Sidney Rigdon, Parley Pratt, and others, that Lucas wanted a peace conference with them. When they met together, however, Lucas instantly ordered his guard to surround the Mormon leaders. Whooping and yelling like bloodhounds let loose upon their prey, they swore oaths and mocked the men throughout the night: "Come, Mr. Smith, show us an angel. Give us one of your revelations. Show us a miracle!"[43]

Parley Pratt wrote, "No pen need undertake to describe our feelings during that terrible night, while there confined—not knowing the fate of our wives and children, or of our fellow Saints, and seeing no way for our lives to be saved except by the miraculous power of God. But, notwithstanding all earthly hopes were gone, still we felt a calmness indescribable. A secret whispering to our inmost soul seemed to say: 'Peace, my sons, be of good cheer, your work is not yet done; therefore I will restrain your enemies, that they shall not have power to take your lives.'"[44]

When General Alexander Doniphan received an order from his superior, Lucas, to execute the prisoners the next morning in the public square, he saved their lives by declaring, "It is cold-blooded murder. I will not obey your order. My brigade shall march for Liberty tomorrow morning, at 8 o'clock; and if you execute these men, I will hold you responsible before an earthly tribunal, so help me God."[45]

Pages 150–51: Far West town site. "Under the dark shadows of the night," wrote Lyman Wight, "General Wilson . . . took me [to] one side, and said . . . 'we have one thing against you, and that is you are too friendly to Joe Smith. . . .' I then told Wilson I believed . . . Joseph Smith to be the most philanthropic man he ever saw . . . a friend to mankind, a maker of peace. . . .' '[Then] your die is cast, your doom is fixed,' replied the general, 'you are sentenced to be shot to-morrow morning on the public square. . . .' 'I answered, Shoot, and be damned."[46]

Above: Two feet of stone, one foot of rocks, then one foot of timber were not enough to keep revelation from entering the mind and heart of the Prophet Joseph Smith at Liberty Jail. Here the Prophet cried out for the Lord and was told that his "afflictions [would] be but a small moment." (D&C 121:7.)

Intimidated by Doniphan's stand, Lucas made plans to take the Church leaders to Richmond for trial. Believing they might be shot, Joseph and the others begged to see their families one more time before they left. "When I entered my house, they clung to my garments, their eyes streaming with tears,"[47] wrote Joseph. Parley P. Pratt said, "The cold rain was pouring down without, and on entering my little cottage, there lay my wife sick of a fever. . . . At her breast was our son Nathan, an infant of three months. . . . I stepped to the bed; my wife burst into tears; I spoke a few words of comfort . . . expressing a hope that we should meet again though years might separate us."[48]

Joseph and the other leaders were taken to Richmond for an agonizing preliminary hearing on charges growing out of the armed hostilities. The prisoners submitted a list of defense witnesses, but these were systematically jailed or driven from the county. Parley Pratt described conditions in the jail as they awaited their trial: "Our ears and hearts had been pained, while we had listened for hours to the obscene jests, the horrid oaths . . . and filthy language of our guards . . . as they recounted to each other their deeds of rapine, murder, robbery, etc., which they had committed among the 'Mormons.' . . . They even boasted . . . of shooting or dashing out the brains of men, women and children.

"I had listened till I became so disgusted, shocked, horrified, and so filled with the spirit of indignant justice, that I could scarcely refrain from rising," when "on a sudden [Joseph] arose to his feet, and spoke in a voice of thunder, or as the roaring lion. . . . 'SILENCE, ye fiends of the infernal pit. In the name of Jesus Christ I rebuke you, and command you to be still; or you or I die THIS INSTANT!' He looked upon the quailing guards . . . who, shrinking into a corner, or crouching at his feet, begged his pardon, and remained quiet till a change of guards."[49]

Falsely accused, the prisoners were cast into a two-story, twenty-two-foot-square stone dungeon with the ironic name of Liberty. For the next four winter months, the Prophet and his friends suffered from bitter cold, unfit food, filthy conditions, and smoke inhalation. On the lower level of the jail, they could not stand upright. But worst of all for the Prophet was his inability to

comfort the Saints and his family, who were barely surviving in Far West and whose faith was being sorely tried. Reports of the Saints from the outside were grim.

Finally, Joseph appealed to the Lord: "O God, where art thou? And where is the pavilion that covereth thy hiding place? How long shall thy hand be stayed, and thine eye, yea thy pure eye, behold from the eternal heavens the wrongs of thy people and of thy servants, and thine ear be penetrated with their cries? Yea, O Lord, how long shall they suffer these wrongs and unlawful oppressions, before thine heart shall be softened toward them, and thy bowels be moved with compassion toward them?" (D&C 121:1–3.)

The Lord answered his plea: "My son, peace be unto thy soul; thine adversity and thine afflictions shall be but a small moment; and then, if thou endure it well, God shall exalt thee on high; thou shalt triumph over all thy foes." (D&C 121:7–8.) From the darkness of the Liberty jail, Joseph wrote, "We glory in our tribulation because we know that God is with us."[50]

The conditions in the Liberty jail were extremely poor. At least once the brethren were given food that was said to be human flesh, or "Mormon beef." They refused to eat it. While Hyrum was in the jail, his wife, Mary Fielding Smith, gave birth to a son and was allowed to bring him here to be blessed. With tenderness, Hyrum named his son after his prisoner-brother: Joseph Fielding Smith. This little baby, born in affliction and conflict, would become the sixth president of the Church and preside over it for seventeen years.

For some, the flight from Missouri was evidence that the Lord had forsaken the Saints. They had lost their property and had suffered sorely. Their Prophet was jailed, with no prospect for relief. Their dreams of the promised Zion as the center place were indefinitely postponed.

In fact, the enemies of the Church must have been sure it had been successfully destroyed, once and for all. Yet from Liberty, a steady Joseph wrote, "Zion shall yet live though she seemeth to be dead." And the Lord said, "If the very jaws of hell shall gape open the mouth wide after thee, know thou . . . that all these things shall give thee experience, and shall be for thy good." (D&C 122:7.) The dungeon walls had not been thick enough to stop the light of revelation as Joseph received this assurance from the Lord: "What power shall stay the heavens? As well might man stretch forth his puny arm to stop the Missouri river in its decreed course, or to turn it up stream, as to hinder the Almighty from pouring down knowledge from heaven upon the heads of the Latter-day Saints." (D&C 121:33.)

For the less steady, Missouri had been a time of sifting. John Corrill was one who had once thrown himself wholeheartedly into the cause. He had not whimpered at the expulsion from Jackson County; he had offered to be whipped or die for the gospel; he had wandered homeless into Clay County; he had stood by the Prophet in all things—and now it was enough. He had lost his faith in Joseph Smith. He wrote, "Calculation after calculation has failed, plan after plan has been overthrown, and our prophet seemed not to know the event till too late. If he said, 'Go up and prosper,' still we did not prosper, but have labored and toiled, and waded through trials, difficulties, and temptations, of various kinds, in hope of deliverance. But no deliverance came."[51]

Others, however, did not give up. In the face of great adversity, they grew in faith and courage. Eliza R. Snow, struggling out of Adam-ondi-Ahman in the dead of winter, was taunted by a militiaman, "Well, I think this will cure you of your faith." Looking him square in the eye, she replied, "No, sir, it will take more than this to cure me of my faith."[52] Then she, with twelve thousand others who felt the same way, trudged eastward to the Mississippi River.

Left: Winter scene looking south into the valley of Adam-ondi-Ahman. The Saints were driven to Illinois from this place and from other of their homes in the bitter winter of 1838 and 1839, leaving their Prophet behind them in jail. Hundreds were killed or died from exposure. As they left, though, they remembered the promise of the Lord that "Zion is the city of our God, and surely Zion cannot fall, neither be moved out of her place, for God is there, and the hand of the Lord is there." (D&C 97:19.)

Above: This forsaken field in the northern part of the state symbolizes the routes of the escaping Saints. Brigham Young said, "The soldiers shot down our oxen, cows, hogs, and fowls, at our own doors, taking part away, and leaving the rest to rot in the streets."[53]

5
NAUVOO: A PATTERN FOR BUILDING THE CITY OF GOD

Missouri wanted the Mormons out, and with key leaders of the Church imprisoned, responsibility for the exodus fell to Brigham Young. On January 26, 1839, Brigham created the Committee on Removal, whose job through the winter and spring was to feed, clothe, and transport the poor. By mid-February, a temporary break in the weather allowed the large-scale migration to begin. Saints, some with oxen teams, made several trips between Caldwell County and the Mississippi River to carry friends out of danger. Several families crowded into a single wagon.

Lands and precious possessions left behind were sold at a pitiful rate, as low as fifty cents an acre. One Saint sold his forty acres for a "blind mare and a clock."[1]

Arrival at the Mississippi was no guarantee of comfort either. Lucy Mack Smith said: "The snow was now six inches deep and still falling. We made our beds upon it and went to rest with what comfort we might under such circumstances. The next morning our beds were covered with snow and much of the bedding under which we lay was frozen. We rose and tried to light a fire, but, finding it impossible, we resigned ourselves to our comfortless situation."[2]

Emma Smith traveled with her four children; she carried two cotton bags under her skirt, containing Joseph's priceless translation of the Bible. When she arrived at the frozen Mississippi, she got out, and, with her children clinging to her, she walked across the river.

The residents of Quincy, Illinois, extended kindness and sympathy to the bedraggled refugees, collecting food for them and offering shelter, but as the thousands of Saints arrived at the banks of the Mississippi, living conditions deteriorated and people slept in the open, in tents, and in shanties.

The question now was what they were to do next. Where were they to go? A land speculator, Isaac Galland, hearing of the plight of the Saints, offered to sell the Church large tracts of land in Iowa and Illinois with long-term financing. Sidney Rigdon thought the Saints ought to scatter as their gathering had been the source of so much hostility, but word came from Joseph at the Liberty jail that they were to build a city again.

Pages 156–57: Lush greenery surrounding the lovely home of Heber C. Kimball in Nauvoo, Hancock County, Illinois. This once swampy, mosquito-infested land was purchased by the Saints with long-term financing and low interest rates. The Prophet Joseph instilled a vision in the people to turn this poor land into the largest city in the state of Illinois.

The eastern shore of the frozen Mississippi River at Quincy, Illinois. At this site, hundreds of Saints spent the bitter winter of 1839. Joseph had been imprisoned at Liberty, Clay County, Missouri, and the scattered Saints looked for refuge here at this town of 1,800 inhabitants. Quincy residents showed kindness to the Saints and looked upon their grave conditions with a degree of charity.

The Prophet and his fellow prisoners had sought for a change of venue to be tried in a place more friendly than western Missouri. Finally, the request was granted, and on their journey to Boone County, Missouri, on April 6, 1839, the guards allowed them to escape. They arrived in Quincy just over two weeks later to much jubilation. Parley P. Pratt, who had been in a different prison, recorded his later reunion with Joseph: "Neither of us could refrain from tears as we embraced each other once more as free men. . . . Father and mother Smith . . . were also overwhelmed with tears of joy and congratulations; they wept like children as they took me by the hand; but, O, how different from the tears of bitter sorrow which were pouring down their cheeks as they gave us the parting hand in Far West."[3]

Eight days after the Prophet's arrival, the Saints made the original purchases of the Iowa tracts and the plats at Commerce, on the horseshoe bend in the river.

In these low-lying fields at the western end of Nauvoo, thousands of Latter-day Saints lived under shanties, tents, wagon boxes, and makeshift shelters against the elements while sickness raged among them. Conditions were so poor they could hardly imagine moving out of their beds of affliction to build another city. Joseph had a different vision for them, but first, through the power of God, he and other of the apostles healed many from their physical afflictions. July 22, 1839, became known as "The Great Day of Healing."

Huddled along either side of the Mississippi River in tents and makeshift shelters, the Saints suffered from malarial fevers that ran rampant among them in July 1839. Many died, and others "were only just barely able to crawl around and wait upon each other."[4]

Then on July 22, "[Joseph] arose from his bed and commenced to administer to the sick in his own house and door-yard, and he commanded them in the name of the Lord Jesus Christ to arise and be made whole; and the sick were healed upon every side of him.

"Many lay sick along the bank of the river; Joseph walked along up to the lower stone house, occupied by Sidney Rigdon, and he healed all the sick that lay in his path. . . .

"The next place they visited was the home of Elijah Fordham, who was supposed to be about breathing his last. . . . The Prophet of God walked up to the dying man and took hold of his right hand and spoke to him; but Brother Fordham was unable to speak, his eyes were set in his head like glass, and he seemed entirely un-

conscious of all around him. . . . Joseph asked him if he had faith to be healed. He answered, 'I fear it is too late; if you had come sooner I think I would have been healed.' The Prophet said 'Do you believe in Jesus Christ?' He answered in a feeble voice, 'I do.' Joseph then stood erect, still holding his hand in silence several moments; then he spoke in a very loud voice, saying, 'Brother Fordham, I command you, in the name of Jesus Christ, to arise from this bed and be made whole.' . . .

"It seemed as though the house shook to its very foundations. Brother Fordham arose from his bed, and was immediately made whole. His feet were bound in poultices which he kicked off; then putting on his clothes he ate a bowl of bread and milk and followed the Prophet into the street."

"Wherefore . . . have miracles ceased? . . . [For] Christ hath said: If ye will have faith in me ye shall have power to do whatsoever thing is expedient in me." (Moroni 7:27, 33.)

Above: Nauvoo was a place of building and activity for seven years. Construction was the main industry—nearly 4,000 homes would be built in the area. The house on the left belonged to Jonathan Browning, whose son became world famous for the manufacture of firearms. The Prophet received a revelation calling for Nauvoo to be a cornerstone of Zion "which shall be polished with the refinement which is after the similitude of a palace." (D&C 124:2.)

Right: Early morning light washes the bucket for the well behind the Webb Blacksmith shop on Parley Street. Homes in the area were built to last, lawns and gardens were manicured, and beautiful fences were placed around properties. Water was abundant, and crops flourished in the rich, dark soil of the Mississippi flood plain.

With an eye of vision that went beyond the malarial swamp, Joseph renamed Commerce *Nauvoo,* a Hebrew word meaning "a beautiful place." The Saints set out to make the place live up to its name.

Colonel Thomas L. Kane, a non-Mormon who, weary with traveling through Iowa, among "a country marred without being improved by [the] careless hands" of the idle settlers, describes his delight at descending a last hillside and having Nauvoo come into view: "Half encircled by a bend of the river, a beautiful city lay glittering in the fresh morning sun. Its bright new dwellings, set in cool green gardens ranging up around a stately dome-shaped hill. . . . The city appeared to cover several miles, and beyond it, in the background, there rolled off a fair country chequered by the careful lines of fruitful husbandry. The unmistakable marks of industry, enterprise and educated wealth everywhere, made the scene one of singular and most striking beauty."[6]

Nauvoo was not going to be a backwoods gathering of hastily thrown up buildings but a substantial city laid out in four-acre blocks, graced by brick and frame homes, a university, and a hotel called the Nauvoo House. Construction was booming, but with the sounds of hammer and saw filling the air, members of the Quorum of the Twelve were called to another mission of building. In Kirtland in 1835, they had been called as "special witnesses of the name of Christ in all the world." (D&C 107:23.) Now in August 1839, they began to leave for Great Britain, having earlier been promised that "in whatsoever place ye shall proclaim my name an effectual door shall be opened unto you, that they may receive my word." (D&C 112:19.)

This was the gospel of Jesus Christ, meant not just for a small group of people in a particular region. It was meant to roll forward, gathering momentum, until it blessed the whole earth, and its organization would follow the ancient pattern—with apostles, prophets, priests, and teachers.

Left: Entry of the Seventies Hall in Nauvoo with period handwoven rugs gracing the floors and the stairs. Christ called "other seventy" to go out two by two to preach the gospel to the regions round about and to help the twelve apostles take His gospel to all the world. (Luke 10:1.) The upper rooms of this lovely building served as the city library and as a small museum.

Above: The warm glow of the sun fills this main-floor meeting room in the Seventies Hall, which was used by the fifteen quorums of seventies in Nauvoo at that time. At the dedication of this beautiful edifice (after Joseph's death), a choir sat on the left and a brass band sat in front. "The excellent melody of the Choir and Band, mingled with the devout aspirations of a congregation of all saints, gave . . . an air of interest, felicity, and glory, at once feeling, touching, pathetic, grand, and sublime."[7]

Several of the apostles arose from malarial sickbeds to leave on their missions for Great Britain. Brigham Young was still so weak he could not walk the five hundred feet to the river without assistance. Vilate, Heber C. Kimball's beloved wife, was in bed, shaking with a chill with two sick children beside her as he left. Heber said to Brother Brigham, "This is pretty tough, isn't it. Let's rise up and give them a cheer." Heber recorded, "We arose, and swinging our hats three times over our heads, shouted 'Hurrah, hurrah for Israel.'"[8]

En route to the East, they often took a coach. Every time Brigham reached inside the trunk for the fare money, he found just enough. He assumed Heber had replenished their cash supplies; however, he later learned that he had not. Their $13.50 in donations as they left Nauvoo paid $87 worth of coach fares. They could only assume the money had been given them by an unseen hand eager to have the gospel of Jesus Christ move forward.

Wilford Woodruff was among the first to arrive in England on this mission, meeting with a people prepared to hear the gospel. He recorded that while preaching in the town of Hanley on the Sabbath, "the spirit of the Lord rested upon me and . . . said to me, 'This is the last meeting that you will hold with this people for many days.'"[9] He was astonished as he had many appointments in the district, but the next morning the Spirit told him to go south.

Taking his journey he came to the farm of John Benbow. He later wrote: "I . . . rejoiced greatly at the news Mr. Benbow gave me, that there was a company of men and women—over six hundred in number—who had . . . taken the name of United Brethren. . . . This body of United Brethren were searching for light and truth . . . and were calling upon the Lord continually to open the way before them and send them light and knowledge, that they might know the true way to be saved."[10] Wilford preached to these people, and all but one were baptized.

The Church experienced phenomenal growth while the apostles labored in England. Through these early efforts, during the next decade nearly ten thousand British converts sailed to America, gathering with the Saints.

Pages 166–67: Looking east from the Heber C. Kimball home to the home of Winslow Farr. Heber Kimball, one of the first apostles of the last days, lived in this home only five months; then he and his family were driven out again to live four years in wagon boxes and makeshift housing.

Above: One of the oldest homes in Nauvoo belonged to Sarah Melissa Granger Kimball. The initial meetings for the Female Relief Society of Nauvoo were held in this home.

Right: Flowers grace the home of Sarah Kimball. As Joseph began to organize the women into an official entity of the Church, he said the group should "move according to the ancient priesthood, . . . choice, virtuous and holy," and that he would make of them "a kingdom of priests as in Enoch's day."[11]

One day, in the spring of 1842, Sarah Granger Kimball and a Miss Cook were talking together and decided they would like to sew some shirts for the poorly clothed men working on the temple. They wondered, too, if their neighbors would like to help, and invited several women to Sarah's home to form a Ladies Society. Eliza R. Snow was asked to write a constitution and by-laws and submit them to Joseph prior to the next meeting.

Eliza cheerfully responded, and when she read them to Joseph, he replied "that the constitution and by-laws were the best he had ever seen. 'But,' he said, 'this is not what you want. Tell the sisters their offering is accepted of the Lord, and He has something better for them than a written constitution.'"[12] He told the sisters to meet in the room over his store the following Thursday afternoon, saying, "I will organize the sisters under the priesthood after a pattern of the priesthood."[13] He further said, "The Church was never perfectly organized until the women were thus organized."[14]

Western light touching a fence in Nauvoo. Joseph taught that "the things of God are of deep import; and time, and experience, and careful and ponderous and solemn thoughts can only find them out. Thy mind, O man! if thou wilt lead a soul unto salvation, must stretch as high as the utmost heavens . . . thou must commune with God. How much more dignified and noble are the thoughts of God, than the vain imaginations of the human heart!"[15]

Throughout Joseph's lifetime, he had seen examples of powerful women exercising mighty faith, and it was surely with this in mind that he organized the Female Relief Society of Nauvoo on March 17, 1842, to look after the needs of the poor and to help correct the morals and strengthen the virtues of the community.

Emma was elected president of the group, and it was she who suggested its name. "We are going to do something extraordinary," Emma told the women. "When a boat is stuck on the rapids with a multitude of Mormons on board, we shall consider that a loud call for *relief*. We expect extraordinary occasions and pressing calls."[16]

They did indeed respond to pressing calls, involving themselves in everything from delivering babies to boarding temple workmen to helping the destitute converts who streamed into Nauvoo. With remarkable strength, Emma rallied a delegation of Relief Society women to the office of Governor Carlin of Illinois, petitioning him to protect Joseph Smith and the Nauvoo Saints.

Addressing the group in April 1842, Joseph "gave a lecture on the priesthood showing how the sisters would come in possession of the privileges, blessings, and gifts of the priesthood, and that the signs should follow them, such as healing the sick, casting out devils, etc., and that they might attain unto these blessings by a virtuous life and conversation and diligence in keeping all the commandments."[17]

A month later, in the same room above his store, thirty-six-year-old Joseph Smith called to his side nine of the most faithful brethren, including Hyrum Smith, Brigham Young, Heber C. Kimball, and others, later including their wives. He had come to a decision.

For some time, Joseph had felt a growing impression from the Spirit that he would not live to see the Nauvoo temple completed. In fact, Brigham Young later said, "I heard Joseph say many a time, 'I shall not live until I am forty years of age.'"[18] To Mary Elizabeth Rollins he had confided, "I must seal my testimony with my blood."[19] Yet a critical part of his work was in restoring the ordinances and principles that entitled men and women to the fulness

of the priesthood and the glorious blessings of exaltation—living forever in the presence of God. The Lord had an endowment of knowledge from on high for his children.

In his anxiety that he wouldn't live, to these chosen few he administered the ordinances so that if anything should happen to him, in the words of John Taylor, "he would feel that he had then fulfilled his mission, that he had conferred upon others all the keys given to him by the manifestations of the power of God."[20]

So, on May 3, the Prophet arranged his office and assembly room to represent the interior of a temple as much as the circumstances would permit.[21] The next day, he said, "I spent the day in the upper part of the store . . . instructing them in the principles and order of the Priesthood, attending to washings, anointings, endowments and the communication of keys pertaining to the [priesthood]."[22] In the next two years, he introduced the endowment to approximately ninety men and women.

Shadows of the afternoon light upon the fall-colored walnut tree are cast upon Joseph Smith's store and office. Here the temple ordinances in their fullness were revealed to Joseph. Here the Relief Society was officially organized. In Nauvoo, seven more revelations were received by Joseph that became canonized in the Doctrine and Covenants. The Lord desires to reveal all things to the children of men that will bring them back into His presence.

Wilford Woodruff's game of "fox and geese" in his home in Nauvoo. Despite Joseph's serious calling as the mouthpiece of God, he loved to play ball with the children at Nauvoo and to be jovial at times. He explained that a hunter could not always keep his bow strung up because it would lose its elasticity. With the pressures he bore, neither could he be always strung so tightly.

Joseph emerged from his months in the Liberty jail with deeper spiritual maturity and power. For nearly nineteen years he had often faced mobs or persecutions, but in prison, though miserable, he had unhindered time to ponder on all the things he had been through and learned. Before the jail, because of his lack of polish and experience, he used great orators to speak for him, like Sidney Rigdon and Oliver Cowdery. Now he would stand on his own.

While visiting in Philadelphia, Joseph was invited to speak in a very large church. Three thousand people crowded to hear him. Sidney Rigdon, by tradition, arose to speak and dwelt on the gospel and illustrated his points through the Bible. "When he was through," recorded Parley Pratt, "brother Joseph arose like a lion about to roar; and being full of the Holy Ghost, spoke in great power, bearing testimony of the visions he had seen, the ministering of angels which he had enjoyed; and how he had found the plates of the Book of Mormon, and translated them by the gift and power of God. He commenced by saying: 'If nobody else had the courage to testify of so glorious a message from Heaven, and of the finding of so glorious a record, he felt to do it. . . . The entire congregation were astounded; electrified, as it were, and overwhelmed with the sense of the truth and power by which he spoke, and the wonders which he related. A lasting impression was made. . . . Multitudes were baptized in Philadelphia and in the regions around."[23]

Joseph gave a characterization of himself, saying, "I am like a huge, rough stone rolling down from a high mountain; and the only polishing I get is when some corner gets rubbed off by coming in contact with something else, striking with accelerated force against religious bigotry, priestcraft, lawyer-craft, doctor-craft, lying editors . . . and jurors . . . backed by mobs, blasphemers, licentious and corrupt men and women—all hell knocking off a corner here and a corner there. Thus I will become a smooth and polished shaft in the quiver of the Almighty."[24]

"His magnetism was masterful, and his heroic qualities won universal admiration," wrote George Q. Cannon. "Where he moved all classes were forced to recognize in him the man of power."[25]

Joseph and Emma Smith Mansion House completed in 1843. Joseph and family, now with four children, moved into the mansion about the end of August. At an "opening" of the house, 100 couples dined together for the evening. More than 10,000 people would view the slain bodies of Joseph and Hyrum in this house. Joseph lived here only ten months.

Western light streams into Joseph's study in the Mansion House. Though his responsibilities often tore him away, Joseph loved the hours at home with his family. On one occasion, in this house, Joseph led some of the apostles and leaders of the Church in prayer and begged the Lord to prolong his days upon the earth, to give him power over all of his enemies, and to bless all the households in Nauvoo, the Church, and the world.

When George Q. Cannon arrived as a young English convert at the dock landing at Nauvoo, "the general conference of the Church was in session and large numbers crowded . . . to welcome the emigrants. . . . [I] sought with a boy's curiosity and eagerness . . . to get sight of the Prophet . . . whom [I] never met. When [my] eyes fell upon the Prophet, without a word from anyone to point him out, . . . [I] knew him instantly. [I] would have known him among ten thousand."[26]

Joseph was stretched by the Lord to do things for which he had never been trained in the temporal sense. Men of affairs who visited Nauvoo in its time of glory—and there were many—were astonished that someone with such little education could accomplish such a breadth of achievements. He was at one time mayor, chief justice, lieutenant-general of the legion, editor of the leading periodical, regent of the university, organizer of industry, and president of the Church. When he preached, there fell from his lips, under the influence of God, doctrines of such incredible originality and spiritual power that people were uprooted from their traditions to come to a new way of thinking.

Still, for all this, Joseph did not tend toward self-aggrandizement. He wrote, "My house has been a home and resting-place for thousands, and my family many times obliged to do without food, after having fed all they had to visitors; and I could have continued the same liberal course, had it not been for the cruel and untiring persecution of my relentless enemies."[27]

Because Joseph was hounded on every side by those enemies, he sometimes went into hiding. Even crouched in the attic of a friend's house, perhaps Edward Hunter's, he could write with a confidence born of absolute knowledge of the Lord who led him: "Shall we not go on in so great a cause? Go forward and not backward. Courage, brethren; and on, on to the victory!" (D&C 128:22.)

Joseph had great compassion for others. Mary Frost Adams recalled: "While he was acting as mayor of the city, a . . . man called Anthony was arrested for selling liquor on Sunday, contrary to law. He pleaded that the reason he had done so was that he might raise the money to purchase the freedom of a dear child held as a slave in a Southern State. He had been able to purchase the liberty of himself and wife and now wished to bring his little child to their new home. Joseph said, 'I am sorry, Anthony, but the law must be observed, and we will have to impose a fine.' The next day Brother Joseph presented Anthony with a fine horse, directing him to sell it, and use the money obtained for the purchase of the child."[28]

Children held a warm place in the prophet's heart. In fact, Mary said that all children loved him, "for he was never so busy but that he always had a kind word and a smile for the little ones."[29]

One evening as he was walking with his bodyguards—and with the threats upon his life, he needed them—Joseph passed a door that was slightly ajar. Inside was a little boy kneeling in prayer, asking that Joseph would be safe from his enemies. The Prophet turned to the guards and said that they might all go to bed and sleep soundly, for the Lord had heard the boy's prayer, and no harm would befall them that night.[30]

The Jonathan Browning cabin is located behind (to the east of) the Browning home and gunsmith shop. There was a loft above this room where the children slept. The inside of this cabin is restored to the simple look of the period. Though there were numerous lovely brick and frame structures, this type of home was most common and would serve well to protect the Saints from the bitterly cold winters and the humid, hot summers.

The first light of the morning sun touches this winter scene of the printing complex in Nauvoo. John Taylor lived in the center building and was the editor of the Times and Seasons. *He also helped to oversee the printing of the Book of Mormon and various periodicals, pamphlets, and other communications. The complex contained a stereotype foundry, typesetting oven, press room, book bindery, and retail bookstore. John Taylor bought this complex and said, "I felt like sacrificing all things when called upon, my heart is not set upon property, but the things of God: I care not so much about the good things of this life, as I do about . . . fulfilling the work the Lord has called me to do."*[31]

Joseph said, "If men do not comprehend the character of God, they do not comprehend themselves."[32] With his visions and heavenly instruction, he came before an unbelieving world with boundless riches in his hands, new vistas of comprehension. He once said, with a bit of irony, that if he were a false teacher, he could "be hailed as a friend, and no man would seek my life."[33] He had instead the burden of being a prophet, teaching in a simple, straightforward, noble manner that left no room for contention.

To the Saints he asked, "What is the object of our coming into existence, then dying and falling away, to be here no more? It is but reasonable to suppose that God would reveal something in reference to the matter. . . . Reading the experience of others, or the revelation given to *them*, can never give *us* a comprehensive view of our condition and true relation to God. . . . Could you gaze into heaven five minutes, you would know more than you would by reading all that ever was written on the subject."[34]

When asked what was unique about Mormonism, he replied that it is the "pure doctrine of Jesus Christ; of which I myself am not ashamed."[35] When Martin Van Buren, then president of the United States, asked how this gospel differed from other religions of the day, Joseph said: "We differed in mode of baptism, and the gift of the Holy Ghost by the laying on of hands. We considered that all other considerations were contained in the gift of the Holy Ghost."[36]

Certainly one of those considerations was the question of authority. As the Lord had said, "Many there be who are under this condemnation, who use the name of the Lord, and use it in vain, having not authority." (D&C 63:62.)

Who can act for the Lord without his permission? Who can baptize? Only those who have been specifically granted that power of authority. To Joseph the Lord had said, "Whatsoever you seal on earth shall be sealed in heaven; and whatsoever you bind on earth, in my name and by my word, saith the Lord, it shall be eternally bound in the heavens." (D&C 132:46.)

Pages 178–79: Winter glow of the western sun upon the windows of the Joseph Coolidge home and the Snow-Ashby Complex (left) on the corner of Parley and Hyde Streets. A German, Mr. Kaufman, placed an inscription on the home after the Mormon exodus that says: "This house is mine and yet not mine. Who comes after me shall find the same. I have been here and who reads this shall also have been here."[37]

Above: The quarry for the temple stone was located just north of town. "There have been frequently, during the winter, as many as one hundred hands quarrying rock, while at the same time multitudes of others have been engaged in hauling, and in other kinds of labor."[38] The walls of the temple were made of solid blocks of cut limestone from four to six feet thick, with some of the stones weighing up to two tons.

"Now brethren," Joseph had promised, "I obligate myself to build as great a temple as ever Solomon did if the church will back me up. Moreover it shall not impoverish any man but enrich thousands."[39] Clearly, Joseph was speaking in eternal terms, for the temple would cost a great fortune for that day—over a million dollars with the faithful giving a tithe (one-tenth) of their time and their income or even much larger consecrations to the temple building. Nauvoo's newspaper *The Times and Seasons* said that not even the widow in many instances could be prevented, "out of her scanty pittance from throwing in her two mites."[40] But the gifts the Lord had for them in return were priceless.

Wherever the Saints had been, they left behind the hope of building a temple where they could receive the crowning jewel of the restored gospel of Jesus Christ—the ordinances available only in this holy house.

Joseph saw in vision what the Nauvoo Temple should look

like, and when architect William Weeks brought him the plans, Joseph asked where the round windows were that should be between the first and second floors to let light stream into the temple. Weeks protested that structurally he thought it impossible to put round windows in that place, for they could not bear the weight of the building above them. To this Joseph answered that he had seen the round windows in the vision, and that that was the way the Lord wanted it to be. They had to find a way to do it.

The cornerstones were laid in a particular order, beginning with the southeast cornerstone as a symbol of the order of the kingdom. With the eyes of a seer, Joseph assured the Saints "that the ancient Prophets beheld and rejoiced at this scene, and are near to witness the fulfillment of their predictions."

"The building up of Zion is a cause that has interested the people of God at every age," reported *The Times and Seasons*. "They have looked with joyful anticipation to the day in which we live."[41]

Southwest corner of the Nauvoo Temple site where there was a circular staircase. The building was constructed after a pattern given to Joseph by the Lord. One day in 1844, while touring the city with Josiah Quincy, Joseph stopped at the temple site by one of the workers carving out the giant sunstones. Josiah recorded, perhaps with tongue in cheek, that the worker turned to Joseph and said, "General Smith, is this like the face you saw in vision?" "Very near it," answered the prophet, "except that the nose is just a thought too broad."[42]

Model of the beautiful Nauvoo Temple, at the location of the original. The temple, constructed from 1841 to 1846, was the most unusual building in all of the western United States at that time. It measured 128 feet in length and 88 feet in width and was 60 feet high at the overhang. The top of the belfry and clock dome rose 158.5 feet off the ground.

Stretching his hand toward the uncompleted temple, Joseph said, "If it should be the will of God that I might live to behold that temple completed and finished from the foundation to the top stone, I will say, 'Oh Lord, it is enough. Lord let thy servant depart in peace.'"[43]

Why this yearning sense of urgency for Joseph to complete the temple? He gives his reasons. To the sisters of the Relief Society, he said, "The Church is not now organized in its proper order, and cannot be until the temple is completed."[44] To the elders he had said, "You need an endowment, brethren, in order that you may be prepared and able to overcome all things."[45]

Brigham Young defined endowment: "Your *endowment* is, to receive all those ordinances in the House of the Lord, which are necessary for you, after you have departed this life, to enable you to walk back to the presence of the Father, passing the angels who stand as sentinels, being enabled to give them the key words, the signs and tokens, pertaining to the Holy Priesthood, and gain your eternal exaltation in spite of earth and hell."[46]

The Lord said that until the temple was built, there was no place on earth where he could come and restore the fulness of the priesthood. (D&C 124:28.) "For," said he, "I deign to reveal unto my church things which have been kept hid from before the foundation of the world." (D&C 124:41.)

Ordinances in the temple were to be done for the living and for the dead. Because God is no respecter of persons, those who have passed from this life without opportunity to be taught the true gospel and given the saving ordinances receive their opportunity in the world of spirits. As the Doctrine and Covenants explains, messengers are commissioned to "go forth and carry the light of the gospel . . . even to all the spirits of men; and thus was the gospel preached to the dead." (D&C 138:30.)

The temple would be the place reserved for humanity to do the work by proxy for those who had passed away, including baptism for the dead. This is one of the mysteries of God known in ancient times that had passed from the earth until the Restoration. The Apostle Paul had asked the Corinthians, "Else what shall they do which are baptized for the dead, if the dead rise not at all? why are they then baptized for the dead?" (1 Corinthians 15:29.)

The Saints felt such anxiety about completing the temple and receiving their ordinances that as conflicts began to heat up with their neighbors and they feared that they would again have to abandon their homes, instead of stopping work on the temple, they stepped up their labors. At one point, Brigham Young said, "Such has been the anxiety manifested by the saints to receive the ordinances (of the Temple), and such the anxiety on our part to administer them, that I have given myself up entirely to the work of the Lord in the Temple night and day, not taking more than four hours sleep, upon an average, per day, and going home but once a week."[47]

After the temple was completed, temple work was done round the clock until the Saints were forced to leave. Joseph would not live to see this day.

There were thirty pilasters on the outside walls of the temple, with a moonstone at the bottom and a sunstone at the top of each and starstones set above the sunstones. Faithful Saints would give one day in ten to the building of the Lord's house, if not more. Skilled converts were arriving nearly every month now, and all wanted to work on this noble building.

Joseph surprised strangers who supposed that a prophet would be sober and sedate, perhaps old and bearded. He had many attractive personal qualities, standing an athletic six feet tall, being robust and outgoing and fond of sports. It was said that nobody could best him at stick pulling or jumping the mark. In fact, his happy nature disgruntled some people.

One day two ministers visited him, trying to corner him in scriptural matters. Unbeaten there, Joseph walked outside, drew a mark on the ground, and jumped. Then he told the ministers that they hadn't bested him at the scriptures, so they might see if they could best him at jumping. They refused, walking away in disgust.[48]

Besides the gospel, Joseph's abiding love was for his family. He and Emma had nine children, of whom three died at birth and another at eleven months. Writing to Emma while away once, he said, "I shall be filled with constant anxiety about you and the children until I hear from you and in a particular manner little Frederick it was so painful to leave him sick. . . . It will be a long and lonesome time during my absence from you and nothing but a sense of humanity could have urged me on to so great a sacrifice."[49]

A man of great integrity, Joseph asked Thomas Colburn in the spring of 1843 if he could borrow $100 to pay the lawyer who had defended falsely accused Porter Rockwell. Said Joseph of the money, "This shall be returned within three days, if I am alive."

After Joseph left, Colburn's sister said to him, "Don't you know, Thomas, you will never see a cent of that money again. Here are your family without a home, and you throw your money away."

"The day came when it was to be paid—a cold, wet, rainy day. The day passed. Night came—9 o'clock, 10 o'clock, and we all retired for the night. Shortly after there was a knock at the door," recorded Colburn's daughter. "Father arose and went to it, and there in the driving rain stood the Prophet Joseph" with the money in gold. He said, "Brother Thomas, I have been trying all day to raise this sum, for my honor was at stake. God bless you."[50]

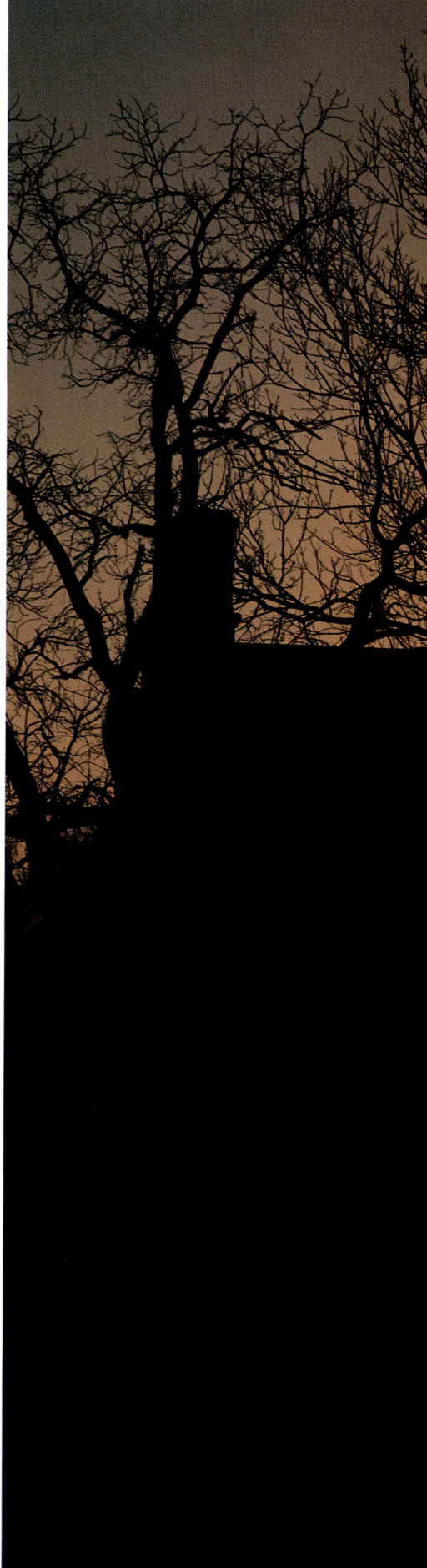

Pages 184–85: Winter sunrise by the Lucy Mack Smith home in Nauvoo. Lucy lost two babies. She saw two sons die of illness, her husband pass away, and three sons killed by mobs. Joseph Smith Sr. said of Lucy, "Mother, do you not know, that you are one of the most singular women in the world?"[51] Lucy lived to the age of 80 and passed away in May 1856.

Above: After the temple was destroyed by fire in 1848 and leveled by a tornado in 1850, locals used the site as a quarry for cut stone to place into their own buildings. This old building in Nauvoo (owned by the American Legion) is made completely from temple stone.

Right: Ominous thunderclouds growing north of Nauvoo, with the home of Brigham Young silhouetted. Brigham said, "I feel like shouting hallelujah, all the time, when I think that I ever knew Joseph Smith."[52]

Joseph once said to his cousin George A. Smith: "Never be discouraged. If I were sunk in the lowest pit of Nova Scotia, with the Rocky Mountains piled on me, I would hang on, exercise faith, and keep up good courage, and I would come out on top."[53] And so it seemed to be for the Prophet at times.

That is the kind of gumption Joseph needed in his prophetic calling, because he was always swimming upstream. As early as 1833, he had led the Saints in seeking redress from the wrongs they had suffered in Missouri, appealing to U. S. President Martin Van Buren for help. Joseph said of the meeting, "I had an interview with Martin Van Buren, the President, who treated me very insolently, and it was with great reluctance he listened to our message, which, when he had heard, he said: *'Gentlemen, your cause is just, but I can do nothing for you.'*"[54]

Years after it was clear the Saints would get no relief from the state, Missouri was an issue that would not die. In May 1842, Lilburn W. Boggs, now the former governor, was seriously wounded by a bullet in an attempted assassination. Former mayor of Nauvoo John C. Bennett, embittered because he had been excommunicated from the Church for adultery, contacted Boggs. He claimed Joseph Smith had asked his bodyguard, Porter Rockwell, to murder the former governor.

When told of the charge, colorful Porter Rockwell said, "I can—and I will—whip any man who tells a cursed lie like that about me."[55] But the charges stuck.

In an agreement with the Missouri Governor, Thomas Carlin of Illinois sent officers to arrest Joseph. Using the power of habeas corpus granted in the Nauvoo Charter, Joseph was temporarily freed, but he had to go into hiding.

In 1842, the charges were dismissed, but Bennett was in Missouri in June of 1843 and revived an old charge against Joseph for treason. Again he was arrested and again freed, but it was clear that Joseph's enemies would never leave him alone. Missouri was just south across the river, Illinois was becoming increasingly threatened by the political power of the Mormons, and, worst of all, just as in the time of Christ, the Church itself had its Judases.

Natural light filters through windows in the circuit courtroom in Springfield, Illinois, where the Prophet Joseph was tried for treason and other accusations. Across the street is the capitol building where the governor, Thomas Ford, had his office. In a small trap door seen in the ceiling of this room above the central bench area, a young attorney sometimes sat observing the court proceedings and could have been there during the Joseph Smith trials. This attorney would later become president of the United States—Abraham Lincoln.

It is difficult to say for certain how many times Joseph was arrested or had lawsuits leveled against him. Brigham Young reported that Joseph was subjected to forty-six lawsuits. Some of these were simply harassments, the equivalent of claiming that he was a disturber of the peace. On one day in Kirtland, July 27, 1837, for instance, six writs were served on the Mormon leader. The Prophet recorded, "We were detained all day by malicious and vexatious law suits. About sun-set I got into my carriage to return home to Kirtland; at this moment the sheriff sprang into the carriage, seized my lines, and served another writ on me."[56] He was apparently acquitted from all these charges.

Joseph assessed the trials this way: "As for the perils which I am called to pass through, they seem but a small thing to me, as the envy and wrath of man have been my common lot all the days of my life; and for what cause it seems mysterious, unless I was ordained from before the foundation of the world for some good end, or bad, as you may choose to call it. Judge ye for yourselves. God knoweth all these things, whether it be good or bad. But nevertheless, deep water is what I am wont to swim in. It all has become a second nature to me; and I feel, like Paul, to glory in tribulation; for to this day has the God of my fathers delivered me out of them all, and will deliver me from henceforth; for behold, and lo, I shall triumph over all my enemies, for the Lord God hath spoken it." (D&C 127:2.)

And Joseph ever remembered the word of the Lord in the Liberty jail concerning trials: "The Son of Man hath descended below them all. Art thou greater than he?" (D&C 122:8.)

Still, life became a burden when at every turn was one more subpoena, one more arrest, one more skirmish with the law. Even the mobs who formed against Joseph and the Saints often did so claiming that the law was on their side. Finally, in 1844, Joseph wrote each of the candidates for president, asking, "What will be your rule of action relative to us as a people should fortune favor your ascension to the chief magistracy?"[57] Of the three who replied, none seemed really interested in their cause. It was as Illinois Governor Ford said: the Mormons were so unpopular that even those politicians elected by their votes "were unwilling to risk their popularity with the people by taking part in their favor."[58]

In the face of this, a movement started in Nauvoo for the Prophet to run for president. It was not so much that Joseph expected to win such a campaign; he often referred to it himself with tongue in cheek. "When I get hold of the eastern papers and see how popular I am," he said, "I am afraid that I shall be elected."[59] Still, in this way, he gave his people a good candidate to vote for, and his ideas on government became widely circulated. A pamphlet bearing his political views suggested: "Let us be . . . one family. . . . Reduce Congress at least two-thirds. Two senators from a state and two members to a million of population will do more business than the army that now occupy the halls of the national legislature. . . . All prisoners should be required to work upon roads, public works, or any place where [they] can be taught wisdom and virtue. . . . Slavery ought to be abolished."[60] His campaign was cut short by his death.

Old wood stove and woodbox in the courtroom at Springfield, Illinois. Here the Prophet heard attorneys argue his case, when it was decided that he could not be taken to Missouri on the claim of being an accessory in the attempted murder of ex-governor Boggs. Joseph had sought for redress for himself and the Saints at every level of the government, local and national, to no avail. He told his mother that he would lay his case before the highest court in heaven.

Billowing clouds cover the skies of autumn at Joseph Smith's farm just east of Nauvoo. Joseph and Hyrum and others rode past this place on their way to Carthage. Parley Pratt recorded: "Had [Joseph] been spared a martyr's fate till mature manhood and age, he was certainly endued with powers and ability to have revolutionized the world in many respects, and to have transmitted to posterity a name associated with more brilliant and glorious acts than has yet fallen to the lot of mortal."[61]

Around Nauvoo, now the largest city in Illinois, tensions and emotions were growing as the storms of adversity began to build to thunderous proportions. As had been experienced before, the locals began to be threatened by the great prosperity of the Mormons.

Many, including Joseph, were aware of plots against his life. Faithful teenagers Dennison L. Harris and Robert Scott had been privy to a movement plotting the assassination of Joseph and had attended three of the secret meetings. At the last, knives were placed on their throats by the anxious murderers threatening their lives if they would not swear to secrecy. Not consenting, they escaped with their lives and ran immediately to Joseph and told him of all the details. He blessed them for their bravery.

The conspiracy that had been building was led by William Law, who just weeks before had been second counselor to Joseph, and Law's brother, Wilson. They rallied about two hundred people against Joseph and desired to bring about his downfall by publish-

ing an opposition newspaper called the *Nauvoo Expositor*. Publishing its first issue June 7, 1844, within the city limits of Nauvoo, the paper accused Joseph, among other things, of teaching false doctrines, vicious principles, blaspheming against God, and grasping for political power.

Joseph Smith, as mayor of Nauvoo, acting under council and municipal law, ordered the destruction of the press, the scattering of the type, and the burning of any remaining newspapers. That decision was based on the precedents of the destruction of twenty other printing presses in Illinois in as many years.

In response to this action, the *Warsaw Signal*, another local anti-Mormon paper, published an editorial: "War and extermination is inevitable! Citizens ARISE, ONE and ALL!!!—Can you stand by, and suffer such INFERNAL DEVILS! to ROB men of their property and RIGHTS, without avenging them. We have no time for comment, every man will make his own. LET IT BE MADE WITH POWDER AND BALL!!!"[62]

For those who thought the restored gospel would die with Joseph, the Lord had a response. In the spring of 1844, Joseph gathered the twelve apostles together to pass on the gospel keys. "The room was filled as with consuming fire, his face was as clear as amber, and he was clothed upon by the power of God.... 'I have had sealed upon my head every key, every power, every principle of life and salvation that God has ever given to any man who ever lived upon the face of the earth.... Now,' said he, addressing the Twelve, 'I have sealed upon your heads every key, every power, and every principle which the Lord has sealed upon my head.... I tell you, the burden of this kingdom now rests upon your shoulders; you have got to bear it off in all the world.'"[63]

Joseph had a growing sense that his candle was flickering out. "Some [have] supposed that 'Brother Joseph' could not die," he had told the Saints, "but this is a mistake. It is true that there [have] been times when I have had the promise of my life to accomplish [certain] things; but, having accomplished those things I have not at present any lease of my life. I am as liable to die as other men."[64]

On June 22, 1844, with threats against Joseph heating up, he said, "The way is open. It is clear to my mind what to do. All they want is Hyrum and myself.... We will cross the river tonight, and go away to the West."[65] Thus, just after midnight, Porter Rockwell rowed Joseph and Hyrum and Willard Richards of the Twelve across the Mississippi to hide out on the island near the Iowa side. Joseph had prophesied years before that "the Saints would continue to suffer much affliction . . . and some of you will live to go and assist in making settlements and build cities and see the Saints become a mighty people in the midst of the Rocky Mountains."[66]

Many called Joseph a coward for leaving. Others encouraged him to return—Governor Ford, who was in Carthage, had given his personal promise for Joseph's safety. Still others asked why he would leave them at this hour of greatest need. Dismayed, Joseph, knowing what would happen if he returned to Nauvoo, said aloud, "If my life is of no value to my friends it is of none to myself."[67]

Left: Summer sunset over the Mississippi River. Joseph and Hyrum and Willard Richards were rowed across by Porter Rockwell in an old leaky skiff. They bailed the boat with their boots to keep from sinking. Joseph had felt to flee to the Rocky Mountains. He and Hyrum, after much discussion, returned to Nauvoo on the 23rd and gave themselves up to the "authorities."

Above: Front door of the Mansion House in Nauvoo. Emma sent word across the river for Joseph to come back, thinking that perhaps the Lord would protect him as He had in the past. Emma had been through all the trials and persecutions with Joseph practically from the beginning. Now she did not want to be separated from him in his desires to go to the Rocky Mountains.

Above: A geranium reaching for the light in the handmade glass window of Wilford Woodruff's home. Ten of the twelve apostles were on missions to the East when Joseph and Hyrum were killed. It was as if the Twelve were protected from the actions of the mob by being called so far away.

Right: One can follow the complete 26 1/2-mile length of the old Carthage Road and "Martyrdom Trail" today if one is brave. The road leads through farmers' fields, over small streams, and finally into Carthage. One can only imagine the scene of this Prophet, the head of the dispensation of the fullness of times, and his beloved brother Hyrum riding to the place of slaughter. Just as in the operation when Joseph was a little boy, Hyrum stayed with Joseph to strengthen and comfort him.

Joseph and Hyrum returned to Nauvoo, knowing that a trial in Carthage, the county seat, lay ahead for the *Expositor* affair. Swollen with sadness, they looked upon their families and cradled them in their arms. Joseph could not refrain from weeping as he looked upon his beloved Emma, four months pregnant, and his four little children clinging to his coat.

Joseph, Hyrum, apostles John Taylor and Willard Richards, and fifteen others started on horseback on the road to Carthage at 6:30 A.M., Monday, June 24. The day was sunny and beautiful in contrast to the rain of late. Pausing by the temple, Joseph looked upon the sacred building not yet completed and out over the city of Nauvoo. His mind and heart full of memories and emotion, he said, "This is the loveliest place and the best people under the heavens; little do they know the trials that await them."[68]

Four miles outside of Nauvoo, the group was met by sixty mounted Illinois militia. They had an order from the governor for the Nauvoo Legion to surrender arms and requested Joseph to come back to Nauvoo to see that this order would be followed. As he went, he prophesied, *"I am going like a lamb to the slaughter, but I am calm as a summer's morning. I have a conscience void of offense toward God and toward all men. If they take my life I shall die an innocent man . . . and it shall be said of me 'He was murdered in cold blood!'"*[69]

Joseph bid another farewell to his family, knowing this would be the last time he would see them. Then the large contingency of men began the 26 1/2-mile journey to Carthage on this hot, humid day. Joseph stopped as they passed his farm and looked a good while. As they continued, he kept looking back, also being able to see the temple in the distance. "If some of you had got such a farm and knew you would not see it any more, you would want to take a good look at it for the last time,"[70] he said.

As they arrived in Carthage just before midnight, the town was in an uproar, and the people rejoiced to see the Mormon prophet. Over fourteen hundred militia had gathered, drinking and brawling a good portion of the day as they awaited the arrival of their prey.

The next morning, the prisoners were paraded before the crowds and mocked and derided. The governor addressed the troops, saying that though the prisoners were dangerous men and perhaps guilty, they were now in the hands of the law.

Charged with treason, Joseph and Hyrum received an order committing them to the Carthage jail. The evening of the 26th of June, Willard Richards, John Taylor, and Dan Jones remained with the Prophet and Hyrum in the jail. The brethren prayed together and read from the Book of Mormon: "Thou hast been faithful; wherefore, thy garments shall be made clean. . . . Thou shalt be made strong, even unto the sitting down in the place which I have prepared in the mansions of my Father." (Ether 12:37.)

Late that evening, Joseph said, "I would like to see my family again," and "I would to God that I could preach to the Saints in Nauvoo once more." As the hours passed, Joseph, restless, whispered to Dan Jones, "are you afraid to die?" Dan said, "Has that time come, think you? Engaged in such a cause I do not think that death would have many terrors." Joseph replied, "You will yet see Wales, and fulfill the mission appointed you before you die."[71]

Dan Jones left the jail the next morning, June 27, to see if he could get further attention and aid from the governor. As he passed Frank Worrell, the officer of the guard, Worrell said, "We have had too much trouble to bring old Joe here to let him ever escape alive, and unless you want to die with him you better leave before sundown. . . . You'll see that I can prophesy better than Old Joe."[72]

That afternoon, around 3:15, being much depressed in spirit, Joseph asked John Taylor if he would sing the hymn "A Poor Wayfaring Man of Grief," to which he complied, singing all seven verses. Greatly moved, Joseph asked John to sing it once more. "In pris'n I saw him next—condemned/To meet a traitor's doom at morn;/The tide of lying tongues I stemmed,/And honored him 'mid shame and scorn./My friendship's utmost zeal to try,/He asked, if I for him would die;/The flesh was weak, my blood ran chill,/But the free spirit cried, 'I will!'"[73]

Pages 196–97: The Carthage jail in Carthage, Hancock County, Illinois, where Joseph and Hyrum were murdered by a mob. As prophesied, Dan Jones did fill his mission to Wales, where, through his efforts, 16,000 people joined the Church. Hyrum was the patriarch for the Church, having been ordained after the death of his father; he was also the assistant president. Assurance and a solemn, written pledge had been given by Governor Thomas Ford to the Prophet that he would be protected in Carthage if he would give himself up.

Above: The mob that killed the Prophet and the Patriarch had painted their faces black to hide their identities. They stormed the jail through this door and ran up these stairs and to their right to begin shooting ruthlessly into the jail room. Hyrum stated, "I have not been absent from [Joseph] at any one time, not even the space of six months."[74]

The jailer had let the prisoners stay in his own bedroom, knowing them to be harmless, but upon hearing the threats of the mob, he suggested that they move into the inner cell where they would be safer in the event of an armed attack. There was tension in the air; a foreboding feeling came over the brethren. When Joseph asked Willard Richards if he would go into the cell with him, Dr. Richards answered: "Brother Joseph you did not ask me to cross the river with you—you did not ask me to come to Carthage—you did not ask me to come to jail with you—and do you think I would forsake you now? But I will tell you what I will do; if you are condemned to be hung for treason, I will be hung in your stead, and you shall go free." Joseph embraced Willard and said with emotion, "You cannot." The doctor replied, "I will!"[75]

Before they could move to the inner cell, some minutes after 5:00 P.M., the prisoners heard a rustling outside the jail, and then shots were fired. The brethren sprang to their feet, preparing for the worst. A mob of more than 100 men, many with faces painted black, had surrounded the jail and broken through the door, rushing up the stairs to do their premeditated deed.

The mob fired muskets into the prisoners' room through the doorway. Elder Richards tried to beat down the barrels with a hickory cane and close the door. A fatal shot came through the door and struck Hyrum on the left side of his nose. He fell backward and said, "I am a dead man!"[76] Three more balls entered his body. Joseph cried out, "Oh dear, brother Hyrum!"[77] Balls were flying in all directions. John Taylor tried to make it to the window and was struck in the chest pocket, where the ball hit his watch, stopping it at 16 minutes and 26 seconds past 5:00.

As John fell, three more balls entered his body, severely wounding him. A shower of balls was pouring through all parts of the room. Joseph ran for the window and tried to escape, but while doing so he was hit in the collarbone and in his right breast, with two other balls entering his back. He leaped through the window, exclaiming, "Oh Lord, my God!"[78] and fell to the ground below. Joseph moved his leg some, closed his eyes, and died.

Above and left: View of the assassins as they fired their deadly balls through the door and into the jailer's bedroom where the four prisoners were staying. The original floor still remains at the jail. In the right panel of the door can be seen the hole made by the ball that killed Hyrum. In this room John Taylor, with his beautiful tenor voice, sang all seven verses of "A Poor Wayfaring Man of Grief" to the Prophet. "I had not power to ask his name;/Whither he went or whence he came;/Yet there was something in his eye/That won my love, I knew not why."[79] Joseph tried to escape through the far window on the left but in the attempt was shot four times.

When Joseph fell to the ground, the mob ran outside to make sure the Mormon Prophet was dead. The men began to holler and howl and cheer for the act. Fully expecting to die within moments, Willard quickly pulled John into the inner cell and covered him with straw and an old mattress, telling him that he wanted him to live to tell the story. The mob soon entered the jail again to come after the two, but as they came up the stairs a loud cry was heard: "The Mormons are coming!"[80] The mob quickly dispersed to the woods in fear of the retaliation.

Miraculously, Willard was unharmed. He remembered well what Joseph had prophesied a year before, that "the time would come that the balls would fly around him like hail, and he should see his friends fall on the right and on the left, but that there should not be a hole in his garment."[81]

Samuel Smith rode in great speed to Carthage to give his brothers aid. He was discovered and chased by the mob. He later told his mother, "I have had a dreadful distress in my side ever since I was chased by the mob."[82] Thirty-three days later, he died.

Elder Richards sent the terrible message to Nauvoo: "CARTHAGE JAIL, 8:05 o'clock, p.m., June 27th, 1844. Joseph and Hyrum are dead. Taylor wounded . . . I am well. Our guard was forced, as we believe, by a band of Missourians from 100 to 200. The job was done in an instant, and the party fled towards Nauvoo. . . . The citizens here are afraid of the Mormons attacking them. I promise them no! W. Richards. John Taylor."[83]

Now, in the short period of less than four years, Lucy Mack Smith had lost her beloved husband and four of her sons, Don Carlos, Hyrum, Joseph, and Samuel. She wrote: "I was swallowed up in the depths of my afflictions . . . my soul was filled with horror past imagination. . . . At that moment how my mind flew through every scene of sorrow and distress which we had passed. . . . I then thought upon the promise which I had received in Missouri [from the Spirit], that in five years Joseph should have power over all his enemies. The time had elapsed and the promise was fulfilled."[84]

Pages 200–201: The summer light of afternoon shining upon the D. J. Bawden sculpture of Joseph (left) and Hyrum, the Martyrs. As published in History of the Church, *Joseph said: "I told Stephen Markham that if I and Hyrum were ever taken again we should be massacred, or I was not a prophet of God. I want Hyrum to live to avenge my blood, but he is determined not to leave me."[85] Few stories in the history of mankind document such a powerful bond between brothers. John Taylor recorded, "In life they were not divided, and in death they were not separated!" (D&C 135:3.)*

Above: The light of morning illuminates flora on the temple lot in Nauvoo. Though the Prophet and Patriarch had been killed, the authority that had been restored to the earth by holy angels had not passed away.

"Joseph Smith, the Prophet and Seer of the Lord," wrote John Taylor, "has done more, save Jesus only, for the salvation of men in this world, than any other man that ever lived in it. In the short space of twenty years, he has brought forth the Book of Mormon . . . and has been the means of publishing it on two continents; has sent the fulness of the everlasting gospel . . . to the four quarters of the earth; has brought forth the revelations and commandments which compose this book of Doctrine and Covenants, and many other wise documents and instructions for the benefit of the children of men; gathered many thousands of the Latter-day Saints, founded a great city, and left a fame and name that cannot be slain." (D&C 135:3.)

A black cloud of gloom fell over the whole city of Nauvoo. Every person mourned at the loss of their Prophet and Patriarch. The bodies were brought back to Nauvoo by Willard Richards and Samuel Smith before crowds of thousands of weeping Saints. On Sunday, June 30, 1844, Mary Ann Angell Young, wife of Brigham, wrote her husband in the East: "We are in great affliction at this time. Our dear [Brother] Joseph Smith and Hyrum [have fallen] victims to a ferocious mob. The great God of the creation only knows whether the rest shall be preserved in safety or not. . . . I hope you will be careful on your way home and not expose yourself to those that will endanger your life. Yours in haste. If we meet no more in this world may we meet where parting is no more. Farewell."[86]

Members of the Twelve scattered about the East all recorded feeling darkness in their souls on the afternoon of the 27th of June. By August 6, 1844, most of the Twelve had arrived back in Nauvoo, and a meeting was planned to determine who should take the leadership of the Church.

Two days later, the Saints met to decide by common consent whom they would support as their leader. Sidney Rigdon stood first and spoke for an hour and a half about his desires to be guardian of the Church and to build the Church up to Joseph.

Then Brigham Young arose. As he gave his brief remarks, he was miraculously transfigured before the people. Benjamin Johnson jumped to his feet, "for in every possible degree it was Joseph's voice, and his person, in look, attitude, dress and appearance was Joseph himself, personified; and I knew in a moment the spirit and mantle of Joseph was upon [Brigham]."[87]

Zina Huntington wrote, "I closed my eyes. I could have exclaimed, I know that is Joseph Smith's voice! Yet I knew he had gone. But the same spirit was with the people."[88]

Though Joseph was missed terribly by all, the Twelve began to lead the Church, with Brigham Young as president of the quorum. As the Saints gathered for the April general conference of the Church in 1845, a measure was put before them to honor the slain Prophet, and by unanimous vote, the name of Nauvoo was changed to The City of Joseph. W. W. Phelps penned these lines: "Praise to the man who communed with Jehovah!/Jesus anointed that Prophet and Seer./Blessed to open the last dispensation,/Kings shall extol him, and nations revere./Hail to the Prophet, ascended to heaven!/Traitors and tyrants now fight him in vain./Mingling with Gods, he can plan for his brethren;/Death cannot conquer the hero again."[89]

EPILOGUE

The American Prophet, Joseph Smith, was dead, but the Kingdom of God did not die with him, for the Head of the Church is Jesus Christ, and He lives!

Persecutions increased in Nauvoo, and soon Brigham Young and the rest of the leaders of the Church knew that they must do as Joseph had prophesied: flee to the Rocky Mountains. Information had been gathered about land in Texas, Oregon (which comprised the whole of the Northwest), and Upper California, a Mexican province of which the Utah territory was a part. This latter option, the eastern part of the Great Basin, seemed the best choice because of its isolation and its size. Joseph had said that the Saints should "hunt out a good location, where we can remove to . . . and where we can build a city . . . and have a government of our own, get up into the mountains, where the devil cannot dig us out."[1]

With mobs rising up and threatening from every side, the Saints hastily prepared to move west. The first wagons left in February 1846, crossing the frozen Mississippi, with thousands upon thousands of Saints following after. The move was called by many the greatest migration of a people in modern times. In the minds of the faithful likely rang words similar to those of Eliza R. Snow at Adam-ondi-Ahman, "It'll take more than this to cure me of my faith."[2]

On a final rise of a hill in Iowa, where the City of Joseph, Nauvoo, could last be seen, the wagons would roll to a stop and the Saints would get out for one last gaze upon their city fair, sorrowing at the loss. Then they would move on—on to a place in the West, they knew not where.

George Whitaker, one of the pioneers, commented about the Saints' trek westward: "It seemed as though there was something more than human nature which caused them to feel so joyful and happy to leave their comfortable homes and to go out in the dead of winter with so many young children, to face the cold and the storms, and not even knowing where they were going. It seemed to me that we must be in possession of some power besides the power of man."[3]

As many as eighty thousand Saints made the journey across the plains from 1846 to 1869, leaving six thousand graves, mostly unmarked, along the lonesome trail. Here was a people who would sing with all their hearts: "Why should we mourn or think our lot is hard?/'Tis not so; all is right./Why should we think to earn a great reward/If we now shun the fight?/Gird up your loins; fresh courage take./Our God will never us forsake;/And soon we'll have this tale to tell—/All is well! All is well!"[4]

Arriving in the Valley of the Great Salt Lake, a land inhabited only by a few Indians, Brigham Young, in prophetic vision, looked upon the vast desert and said, "It is enough. This is the right place." As he began to lay out the city of Salt Lake, he thrust his cane into the ground and said, "Here we will build the temple of our God."[5] He added, "Some say, '. . . we never began to build a Temple without the bells of hell beginning to ring.' I want to hear them ring again!"[6]

Daniel of old said, "The God of heaven [shall] set up a kingdom, which shall never be destroyed: and the kingdom shall not be left to other people . . . and it shall stand for ever." (Daniel 2:44.)

The ancient prophet Isaiah said: "It shall come to pass in the last days, that the mountain of the Lord's house shall be established in the top of the mountains, and shall be exalted above the hills; and all nations shall flow unto it. And many people shall go and say, Come ye, and let us go up to the mountain of the Lord, to the house of the God of Jacob; and he will teach us of his ways, and we will walk in his paths." (Isaiah 2:2, 3.)

Here was a people who would continue to prosper and look to the counsel of a living prophet, as in the days of old, for guidance of the Lord. "We believe all that God has revealed," Joseph wrote, "all that he does now reveal, and we believe that he will yet reveal many great and important things pertaining to the Kingdom of God." (Article of Faith 9.) Continuing revelation was paramount to this people. While Joseph was imprisoned within a dark dungeon with walls four feet thick in Liberty, Missouri, the Lord said to him: "What power shall stay the heavens? As well might man stretch forth his puny arm to stop the Missouri river in its decreed course, or to turn it up stream, as to hinder the Almighty from pouring down knowledge from heaven upon the heads of the Latter-day Saints." D&C 121:33.)

The work of building up the kingdom of God on the earth continues with thousands of missionaries going into nations of the earth and the islands of the sea, sounding the trumpet, or teaching the word of God, in every ear, striving to take the gospel message to the uttermost parts of the earth. From the humble first printing of the Book of Mormon of 5,000 copies and a mortgaged farm to pay the bill, to the printings of today where the presses run daily and millions of copies are distributed each year in four-score and more languages, the work moves forward.

Just as Joseph of Egypt was separated from his brethren and became the means of saving the house of Israel and Egypt (a type of the world) in former days from starvation, this record of the lineage of Joseph, the Book of Mormon, is the means for saving the people and the house of Israel in the last days.

And this Joseph Smith, an Elias for the second coming of Jesus Christ, has been an instrument in His hands, restoring all the truths that were lost from the earth, for a people must be prepared to meet the Savior Jesus Christ when He comes again. Living prophets lead the way, and an ancient record, the Book of Mormon, stands as a witness to all the inhabitants of the earth that God the Father does live, that Jesus Christ is His Holy Son, the Savior of the world, and that Joseph Smith is indeed a prophet of God.

The small group of believers who met in 1830 in a log house in New York became the beginning of "the stone that was cut out of the mountain without hands" (Daniel 2:34, 25), a kingdom not set up by men, that is rolling forth to become a great mountain that will fill the earth.

NOTES

Spelling, capitalization, and punctuation in quotations have sometimes been modernized for ease of reading.

PROLOGUE

1. Joseph Smith, *History of the Church of Jesus Christ of Latter-day Saints*, 2nd ed. rev., edited by B. H. Roberts, 7 vols. (Salt Lake City: The Church of Jesus Christ of Latter-day Saints, 1932–51), 6:317. (Hereinafter referred to as *HC*.)
2. Joseph Smith–History 1:25.
3. *The life of Thurlow Weed* (Boston: Houghton, Mifflin and Co., 1884), 1:359.
4. Parley P. Pratt, *Autobiography of Parley P. Pratt* (Salt Lake City: Deseret Book Co., 1938), p. 45. (Hereinafter referred to as *PPP*.)
5. Josiah Quincy, *Figures of the Past from the Leaves of Old Journals* (Boston: Roberts Brothers, 1884), p. 376.

SECTION 1
FOUNDATIONS OF FAITH: THE NEW ENGLAND HERITAGE

1. Tunbridge Town Records, Book 1, Town Clerk's Office, Tunbridge, Orange County, Vermont.
2. George A. Smith, "Memoirs," p. 2, Brigham Young University Special Collections.
3. *Journal of Discourses*, 26 vols. (London: Latter-day Saints' Book Depot, 1854–86), 5:102. (Hereinafter referred to as *JD*.)
4. Lucy Mack Smith, *History of Joseph Smith*, reprint (Salt Lake City: Bookcraft, 1958), p. 34. (Hereinafter referred to as *LMS*.)
5. Ibid.
6. Ibid.
7. Ibid., p. 31.
8. Ibid., p. 36.
9. Ibid., p. 49.
10. Ibid.
11. *HC* 4:191.
12. As quoted in *Blessed by Light: Visions of the Colorado Plateau*, edited by Stephen Trimble (Layton, Utah: Peregrine Smith Books, 1986), p. v.
13. *LMS*, p. 67.
14. Ibid.
15. Joseph Smith, *The Papers of Joseph Smith, Volume 1: Autobiographical and Historical Writings*, edited by Dean C. Jessee (Salt Lake City: Deseret Book Co., 1989), p. 5. (Hereinafter referred to as *Papers*.)
16. *LMS*, p. 51.
17. Ibid., p. 55.
18. Ibid., p. 56.
19. Ibid., p. 57.
20. Ibid.
21. Ibid., p. 58.
22. Ibid., p. 59.

SECTION 2
LIGHTS FROM THE HEAVENS AND A VOICE FROM THE DUST

1. *Papers*, p. 268, n. 1.
2. See *Papers*, pp. 5–6.
3. Ibid.
4. Orson Pratt, *An Interesting Account of Several Remarkable Visions and of the Late Discovery of Ancient American Records* (New York: n.p., 1841), pp. 4–5.
5. *Papers*, p. 272.
6. Ibid.
7. Ibid.
8. *HC* 4:536.
9. *Papers*, p. 272.
10. Ibid., p. 6.
11. Ibid., pp. 272–73.
12. Ibid., pp. 6–7.
13. Ibid., p. 273.
14. *HC* 4:536.
15. *Papers*, p. 273, n. 1.
16. Ibid., p. 7.
17. Ibid., pp. 273–74.
18. Joseph Smith–History 1:23–25.
19. *LMS*, pp. 67–68.
20. *Papers*, pp. 276–80.
21. Ibid., p. 281.
22. Ibid., pp. 281, 282.
23. *LMS*, p. 82, 83.
24. Ibid., p. 333.
25. Ibid., p. 87.
26. Ibid., p. 333.
27. Ibid., p. 86.
28. Ibid., p. 89.
29. Ibid., p. 93.
30. *LMS*, p. 81.
31. See F. Richard Hauck, *Deciphering the Geography of the Book of Mormon* (Salt Lake City: Deseret Book Co., 1988), pp. 153–54.
32. *LMS*, p. 102.
33. Ibid., p. 110.
34. *Papers*, p. 285.
35. *LMS*, pp. 128–29.
36. Ibid., p. 129.
37. *HC* 1:43.
38. *Papers*, p. 29.
39. Ibid., p. 30.
40. Ibid., pp. 30–31.
41. *HC* 1:40.
42. Ibid., pp. 31–32.
43. *Kansas City Journal*, June 5, 1881, cited in *Millennial Star* 43 (July 4, 1881): 422–23 and *Millennial Star* 40 (Dec. 9, 1878): 772. See also Journal of Edward Stevenson, Feb. 9, 1886, pp. 32–37, Church Archives.
44. Statement of Emma Smith to her son, Joseph Smith III, Feb. 1879, cited in *The Saints' Herald* 26 (Oct. 1, 1879): 289, 290. See also Joseph Smith III, "Last Testimony of Sister Emma," *Saints Advocate* 2 (Oct. 1879): 52.
45. David Whitmer, *An Address to All Believers in Christ* (Richmond, Mo.: David Whitmer, 1887), pp. 11–12.
46. Journal of Reuben Miller, 1848, and *Millennial Star* 21 (Aug. 20, 1859): 544.
47. *Millennial Star* 40 (May 2, 1878): 772–73.
48. Ibid. See also *Historical Record* 7 (Oct. 1888): 621.
49. See "Newel Knight's Journal," *Scraps of Biography: Tenth Book of the Faith-Promoting Series* (Salt Lake City: Juvenile Instructor Office, 1883), p. 65.
50. *Papers*, p. 296. See also *Times and Seasons* 3 (Sept. 1, 1842): 897–98.
51. *Papers*, pp. 296–97.
52. *LMS*, p. 152.
53. *HC* 1:76, footnote.
54. *Laws of New York* (Albany, N.Y.: H. C. Southwick Co., 1813), pp. 212–19.
55. *JD* 3:91.
56. *PPP*, p. 42.
57. Ibid., p. 24.
58. Ibid., pp. 36–37.
59. Ibid., pp. 37–39.
60. Ibid., pp. 41–42.

SECTION 3
OUT OF POVERTY: A HOUSE FOR THE SON OF GOD

1. *PPP*, p. 47.
2. *Times and Seasons*, 4 (Sept. 1, 1843): 289–90.
3. *PPP*, pp. 47–48.
4. John Murdock, "A Brief Synopsis of the Life of John Murdock taken from an Abridged Record of his Journal," pp. 9–11, in possession of Karl Ricks Anderson. See Karl Ricks Anderson, *Joseph Smith's Kirtland* (Salt Lake City: Deseret Book Co., 1989), p. 6.
5. *History of Geauga and Lake Counties, Ohio* (Philadelphia: n.p., 1878), p. 246. Description is given by Christopher Gore Crary, an early settler of the area, who arrived in Kirtland in May 1811.
6. *Saints' Herald* 29:192.
7. *HC* 1:146, footnote.
8. Ibid.
9. Ibid., 1:215–16, footnote.
10. Ibid.
11. "Philo Dibble," *Juvenile Instructor* 27 (May 15, 1892): 303–4.
12. *Papers*, p. 372.
13. *HC* 1:252.
14. *Papers*, pp. 367–68.
15. Explanatory Introduction of *The Doctrine and Covenants of The Church of Jesus Christ of Latter-day Saints* (Salt Lake City: The Church of Jesus Christ of Latter-day Saints, 1981).
16. *HC* 1:235.
17. *Papers*, p. 367.
18. *HC* 1:262.
19. Ibid., 1:263.
20. Ibid.
21. Ibid., 1:264.
22. Ibid., 1:468.
23. See Anderson, *Joseph Smith's Kirtland*, p. 34.
24. *PPP*, p. 62.
25. *HC* 2:170.
26. *HC* 6:317.
27. *JD* 12:158.
28. Ibid.
29. *Des Moines Daily News*, Des Moines, Iowa, Oct. 16, 1886, as quoted in Paul H. Peterson, *An Historical Analysis of the Word of Wisdom*, Master's Thesis, 1972, Brigham Young University, Provo, Utah, p. 20.
30. Minutes of the St. George (Utah) School of the Prophets, Dec. 23, 1883.
31. *JD* 10:165.
32. Letter from Joseph Smith to William W. Phelps, Jan. 11, 1833, in Joseph Smith, *The Personal Writings of Joseph Smith*, compiled and edited by Dean C. Jessee (Salt Lake City: Deseret Book Co., 1984), p. 263. (Hereinafter referred to as *Personal Writings*.)
33. Eliza R. Snow, *Eliza R. Snow, an Immortal* (Salt Lake City: Nicholas G. Morgan, Sr., Foundation, 1957), p. 54.
34. *LMS*, p. 230.
35. Truman O. Angell, Journal, Manuscript, p. 4, Special Collections, Lee Library, Brigham Young University.

36. "A Brief History of Artemus Millet," Millet Family History, Manuscript, pp. 70, 71, Church Archives.

37. *Times and Seasons* 6 (Jan. 15, 1845): 771.

38. Benjamin F. Johnson, *My Life's Review* (Independence, Mo.: Zion's Printing and Publishing Co., 1947), pp. 15–16.

39. Andrew Larson, *Erastus Snow* (Salt Lake City: University of Utah Press, 1971), p. 466.

40. *Millennial Star*, 25:439.

41. *HC* 2:399.

42. *Times and Seasons* 6 (Apr. 15, 1845): 867.

43. *LMS*, p. 231.

44. *HC* 2:415.

45. Ibid., p. 416.

46. Ibid., p. 426.

47. Ibid., pp. 386–87.

48. Ibid., p. 428.

49. Edward W. Tullidge, *The Women of Mormondom* (New York: Tullidge and Crandall, 1877), p. 95.

50. Ibid., p. 207.

51. "History of Brigham Young," *Deseret News*, Feb. 10, 1858, p. 386.

52. *HC* 2:487.

SECTION 4
MISSOURI: LOOKING FOR THE HIGH GROUND THROUGH THE REFINER'S FIRE

1. *PPP*, pp. 50–51.
2. Ibid., p. 52.
3. *HC* 1:189.
4. Ibid., p. 197.
5. *PPP*, p. 93.
6. Ibid., p. 101.
7. Ibid., pp. 99–100.
8. *Times and Seasons* 4:264.
9. Emily M. Austin, *Mormonism; or, Life Among the Mormons* (Madison, Wis.: M. J. Cantwell, 1882), pp. 72–73.
10. Elizabeth Haven Barlow to Elizabeth Howe Bullard, cited in Kenneth W. Godfrey, Audrey M. Godfrey, and Jill Mulvay Derr, *Women's Voices: An Untold History of the Latter-day Saints, 1830–1900* (Salt Lake City, Deseret Book Co., 1982), p. 109.
11. *PPP*, pp. 107–8.
12. Ibid., p. 108.
13. Ibid., p. 102.
14. *HC* 2:70.
15. Ibid.
16. Matthias F. Cowley, *Wilford Woodruff: History of His Life and Labors* (Salt Lake City: Bookcraft, 1979), p. 39.
17. As quoted in *Conference Report*, April 1898, p. 57.
18. *HC* 2:67, footnote.
19. Cowley, *Wilford Woodruff*, p. 40
20. *HC* 2:71.
21. Ibid., p. 73.
22. Ibid., p. 104, footnote.
23. Ibid., pp. 104–5.
24. Ibid., p. 105.
25. Ibid., p. 116, footnote.
26. Ibid., p. 182.
27. Ibid., 3:328–29.
28. George Q. Cannon, *Life of Joseph Smith the Prophet* (Salt Lake City: Deseret Book Co., 1986), p. 260.
29. *History of Caldwell and Livingston Counties* (St. Louis, Mo.: National Historical Co., 1886), p. 121.
30. *PPP*, p. 173.
31. *HC* 4:163–64.
32. *PPP*, p. 174.
33. *LMS*, pp. 254–56.
34. *Missouri: A Guide to the "Show Me" State*, rev. ed. (New York: Hastings House, 1954), p. 510.
35. *HC* 3:57.
36. *LMS*, p. 261.
37. *HC* 3:163.
38. Ibid., p. 157.
39. Ibid., p. 175.
40. *PPP*, p. 182.
41. Amanda Barnes Smith, Autobiography, Typescript, p. 4, Church Archives.
42. Mercy Rachel Thompson, Autobiography, Typescript, p. 3, Church Archives.
43. *PPP*, p. 187.
44. Ibid., p. 188.
45. *HC* 3:190–91, footnote.
46. *Times and Seasons* 4:267.
47. *HC* 3:193.
48. *PPP*, pp. 189–90.
49. Ibid., pp. 210–11.
50. *Personal Writings*, p. 375.
51. As quoted in John Henry Evans, *Joseph Smith, an American Prophet* (Salt Lake City: Deseret Book Co., 1989), p. 141.
52. Eliza R. Snow, "Sketch of My Life," microfilm of holograph, Church Archives.
53. *Times and Seasons* 4:261.

SECTION 5
NAUVOO: A PATTERN FOR BUILDING THE CITY OF GOD

1. *History of Caldwell and Livingston Counties*, p. 142.
2. *LMS*, pp. 296–97.
3. *PPP*, p. 293.
4. "A Leaf from an Autobiography," *Woman's Exponent*, Nov. 15, 1878, p. 91.
5. *HC* 4:3–4, footnote.
6. Thomas L. Kane, "Address before the Historical Society of Philadelphia," in *Memoirs of John R. Young, Utah Pioneer, 1847* (Salt Lake City: Deseret News, 1920), pp. 31–32.
7. Dean C. Jessee, "The John Taylor Nauvoo Journal," Jan. 1845–Sept. 1845, *BYU Studies*, Summer 1983, p. 7.
8. Orson F. Whitney, *Life of Heber C. Kimball* (Salt Lake City: Bookcraft, 1978), p. 266.
9. Cowley, *Wilford Woodruff*, p. 116.
10. Ibid., p. 117.
11. Andrew F. Ehat and Lyndon W. Cook, *The Words of Joseph Smith* (Provo, Utah: Religious Studies Center, Brigham Young University, 1980), p. 110. (Hereinafter referred to as *Words of Joseph Smith*.)
12. Relief Society of the Church of Jesus Christ of Latter-day Saints, *History of Relief Society: 1842-1966* (Salt Lake City: The General Board of Relief Society, 1966), p. 18.
13. Ibid.
14. Ibid.
15. *HC* 3:295.
16. Minutes of Female Relief Society of Nauvoo, Mar. 17, 1842, Manuscript, Church Archives.
17. *Words of Joseph Smith*, p. 119.
18. *JD* 18:361.
19. Journal of Mary Elizabeth Rollins Lightner, p. 7, Brigham Young University Special Collections.
20. *JD* 25:183.
21. *Deseret News*, Feb. 13, 1884, p. 49.
22. *HC* 5:1–2.
23. *PPP*, pp. 298–99.
24. *HC* 5:401.
25. Cannon, *Life of Joseph Smith*, p. 20.
26. Ibid., pp. 20–21, footnote.
27. *HC* 6:33.
28. *Young Woman's Journal* 17:538.
29. Ibid.
30. Diary of Oliver B. Huntington, vol. 2, pp. 167–68, Brigham Young University Special Collections.
31. Jessee, "The John Taylor Nauvoo Journal," pp. 47–48.
32. *HC* 6:303.
33. Ibid., p. 304.
34. Ibid., p. 50.
35. Ibid., 5:156.
36. Ibid., 4:42.
37. As quoted in Richard Holzapfel and T. Jeffery Cottle, *Old Mormon Nauvoo, 1839–1846* (Provo, Utah: Grandin Book Co., 1990), p. 91.
38. *HC* 4:608.
39. *Words of Joseph Smith*, p. 418.
40. *HC* 4:609.
41. Ibid.
42. Quincy, *Figures of the Past*, p. 389.
43. *Words of Joseph Smith*, p. 418.
44. Ibid., p. 115.
45. *HC* 2:309.
46. *JD* 2:31.
47. *HC* 7:567.
48. Edwin F. Parry, comp. *Stories about Joseph Smith the Prophet* (Salt Lake City: Deseret News Press, 1934), pp. 17–18.
49. *Personal Writings*, p. 448.
50. *Young Woman's Journal*, December 1906, pp. 539.
51. *LMS*, p. 313.
52. *JD* 3:51.
53. As quoted in Evans, *Joseph Smith, an American Prophet*, p. 9.
54. *HC* 4:80.
55. Affidavit of John C. Bennett, sworn before Samuel Marshall, justice of the peace, Hancock County, Illinois, July 7, 1842. Published in *The Wasp*, July 27, 1842.
56. *HC* 2:502.
57. Ibid., 6:65.
58. As quoted in Evans, *Joseph Smith, an American Prophet*, p. 185.
59. Ibid., p. 186.
60. Ibid., pp. 186, 188.
61. *PPP*, p. 46.
62. *Warsaw Signal*, June 12, 1844, p. 2.
63. *Deseret Weekly News*, March 19, 1892, p. 406.
64. *Words of Joseph Smith*, p. 112.
65. *HC* 6:545–46.
66. Ibid., 5:85.
67. Ibid., 6:549.
68. Ibid., p. 554.
69. Ibid., p. 555.
70. Ibid., p. 558.
71. Ibid., p. 601.
72. Letter from Dan Jones to Thomas Bullock, Jan 20, 1855, as quoted in "The Martyrdom of Joseph and Hyrum Smith," *BYU Studies*, Winter 1984, p. 102.
73. *HC* 6:615.
74. *LMS*, p. 259.
75. *HC* 6:616.
76. Ibid., p. 617–18.
77. Ibid., p. 618.
78. Ibid.
79. Ibid., p. 614.
80. Ibid., p. 621.
81. Ibid., p. 619.
82. *LMS*, p. 82.
83. *HC* 6:621–22.
84. *LMS*, p. 325.
85. *HC* 6:546. See also letter of Stephen Markham to Wilford Woodruff, June 20, 1856, Church Archives.
86. Letter of Mary Ann Angell Young in Nauvoo, dated June 30, 1844, to her husband, Brigham Young, Church Archives.
87. Johnson, *My Life's Review*, p. 104.
88. Zina Huntington as quoted in Tullidge, *Women of Mormondom*, pp. 326–27.
89. *Hymns of The Church of Jesus Christ of Latter-day Saints* (Salt Lake City: The Church of Jesus Christ of Latter-day Saints, 1985), no. 27.

EPILOGUE

1. *HC* 6:222.
2. Snow, "Sketch of My Life," Church Archives.
3. George Whitaker, "Life of George Whitaker, a Utah Pioneer, 1820–1907," Typescript, p. 12, Church Archives.
4. *Hymns*, no. 30.
5. In "Pioneers' Day," *Deseret Evening News*, July 26, 1880, p. 2.
6. *JD* 8:355.

"No unhallowed hand can stop the work from progressing;

persecutions may rage, mobs may combine,

armies may assemble, calumny may defame,

but the truth of God will go forth boldly, nobly, and independent,

till it has penetrated every continent, visited every clime,

swept every country, and sounded in every ear,

till the purposes of God shall be accomplished,

and the Great Jehovah shall say

the work is done."

—Joseph Smith the Prophet